INVESTING FOR EVERYONE

Everything you need to know to become a great investor.

Kerim Derhalli

Copyright © 2020 Kerim Derhalli

All rights reserved

No part of this book may be reproduced, or stored in a retrieval system, or transmitted in any form or by any means, electronic, mechanical, photocopying, recording, or otherwise, without express written permission of the publisher.

Cover design by: Invstr Ltd.

This book is dedicated to my parents who gave me an enduring belief in people and what we are all capable of achieving when we work with love and with purpose.

CONTENTS

Title Page
Copyright
Dedication
Preface
MODULE ONE   1
MODULE TWO   9
MODULE THREE   19
MODULE FOUR   29
MODULE FIVE   58
MODULE SIX   78
MODULE SEVEN   93
MODULE EIGHT   105
MODULE NINE   121
MODULE TEN   136
GLOSSARY   144
About The Author   235

PREFACE

Investing is about the future. It is about doing things today that will help give us the future we want. This is as true of our money as it is of our careers and our human relationships. The more we invest in things that matter to us, the more likely we are to fulfill our potential and be truly happy.

When it comes to financial investing, I believe that we are all natural investors. Financial markets are fundamentally about people and human emotions, things that we naturally understand from birth. We can learn to invest in the same way we learn a sport or a musical instrument. We need to get financially fit by following the news, seeing how the markets react and understanding why people behaved that way, practicing our investing (playing with paper money or Fantasy Finance® on the Invstr app), and then going and performing with real investments.

Get Fit, Practice, Perform. It's a simple formula.

This book aims to provide all the theory that anyone practically needs to become a competent and confident investor. It starts at the very beginning, assuming little or no knowledge of investing or the financial markets. It then goes step by step, building on all the key concepts and theories you need to understand.

I have written it in plain English and have avoided the use of jargon. I want to make it as easy as possible for you to learn, not show off my knowledge of long words.

This book is part of what you will need to become a great investor. Imagine you wanted to learn how to cook a meal - you would need the recipe, the ingredients, and a kitchen to cook it in. You can think of this book as the financial recipe. The ingredients you need are the financial data and information to make smart decisions. The kitchen is where you bring your investments to life.

You can find all the financial information you need and a place to buy and sell investments in the free Invstr app, available on iOS and Android. I highly recommend you download it, if you haven't already!

Much like this book, I created Invstr in order to help aspiring investors learn to invest. I've structured the app around three basic principles, which I think are key to smart investing:

Play

On Invstr, we like to make investing fun. One of our biggest components is Fantasy Finance, a portfolio management game where players get $1M in virtual cash to invest in whatever they like. It's just like investing in the real stock market, but without risking any cash. This means that you can practice and experiment without losing any real money.

Just to add in a little friendly competition, we've also created the Invstr Fantasy Leagues, monthly competitions where players can see how their portfolio stacks up against others. Those with portfolios in the Top 25 at the end of each month win real cash prizes and bragging rights!

Learn

As I mention in the book, knowledge is one of the most powerful things you can have when it comes to investing. We take that seriously at Invstr: we offer Invstr Academy, which contains 85 lessons on investing (complete with quizzes, a searchable glossary, and audio recordings for on-the-go learning), daily and biweekly investing podcasts, market news, and live updates. The

Invstr app also streams real-time data and gives you access to charts, technical analysis, and more, so you're always on top of the markets.

The other way we like to learn is from other people. That's why we've built an entire social network within Invstr - member profiles, a social feed, private groups, and direct messaging - so we can learn from each other in a fun and social way.

Invest

As you learn more about investing and practice with Fantasy Finance, you will also want to start investing for real. That's where Invstr+ comes in: a banking, brokerage, and crypto account all in one. Invstr+ allows you to start investing in your favorite companies from as little as $1, but you won't have to do it alone - Invstr Stats and Portfolio Builder combines data and statistical and factor analysis to give you personalized suggestions based on your investment behavior. By getting live feedback and insight into your portfolio and performance, I hope you will also feel empowered to make better investment choices.

You can download Invstr by searching "Invstr" in the App Store or Google Play. You can also follow us on Instagram (@invstr) and Twitter (@invstreams). Need investing news and advice on the go? Listen to Invstr "In the Green" and Invstr "Crunch," our weekly and daily podcasts on investing and finance, available on Apple Podcasts and Spotify.

Whatever stage you are at in your investing journey, I hope that this book and the Invstr app will help you Take Charge of your financial future and Make Change for a financially healthy and sustainable world.

MODULE ONE

Investing Introduction

Lesson One: Introduction

Want to become a better investor? You've come to the right place.

Financial markets reflect everything that's going on in the world. When you learn to invest, you get to understand the present and start taking control of your future. Powerful stuff.

This book teaches you everything you need to know about investing. But this isn't your boring finance textbook. Everything here is short, simple, and sweet. By the end, you're going to be an investing legend.

If you haven't already, I highly recommend downloading the Invstr app in order to fully benefit from what you'll learn in this book. We'll be using Invstr to apply the concepts you've learned in each lesson.

Lesson Two: The Power of Compounding

Imagine this scenario:

You're twenty years old. A relative gives you $10,000. Awesome, right?!

There are a few things you could do. You could spend it. You could save it. Or you could start to invest it.

Let's say you go with option three. What happens if you decide to invest it today? At a 10% annual return, you'll end up with over $1,250,000 when you retire in 50 years - over 100x what you started with!

But if you choose to delay investing until 10 years from now, the $1,250,000 shrinks to less than $500,000. If you choose to start investing 20 years from now, you'll end up with just $191,000.

Why? Because investments grow in value over time. The longer we allow them to grow, the larger they get on their own. The larger they get on their own, the quicker they grow. That's the power of compounding. It's how your money can make you more money.

This is why choosing to invest now is crucial. The sooner we start to invest, the more money we'll earn, and the less money we'll need to invest throughout our lives.

Lesson Three: What is Investing?

Investing is about taking calculated risks in order to achieve a better future. It lets you take control of your money, pay down debts, and create the financial future you want.

It's easy to confuse investing with all the other ways you might make and/or manage your money. Let's walk through how investing differs from your income, saving, trading, and gambling…

Investing vs. Income

Income is money you receive that you don't need to give back. This can include:

- Gifts
- Scholarships
- Financial support under various government assistance programs
- Money you earn from working
- Interest on money in a savings account
- Lottery winning

Income can be earned (money you get from a job) or unearned (money you get without working). When you have income, you can use it however you want, whether it's through spending or saving.

Investing vs. Saving

Saving is keeping your money in reserve instead of spending it, usually in a bank.

Is it safer to put your money in a bank? Usually, yes. But when you only save money instead of investing it, that money will grow very slowly.

When we want to generate a higher rate of return, we usually have to take more risk. We do this by investing in things that normally increase in value over time, like stocks, bonds, commodities, and cryptocurrencies. (You can also make money when you "short" a stock, but we'll get to that later.)

Investing vs. Trading

Trading is opportunistic and reactive: you respond and act depending on the market in a certain time frame

For example: You see someone selling a T-shirt for $10, but you know it's really worth $15. You buy the T-shirt and quickly sell it at $15 for a $5 profit. Swish. You've just made a baller trade.

Investing is different. It's about generating returns consistently over a longer period of time. You'll need patience, careful planning, and money management skills, all of which you'll develop over time. Think of it as a marathon, not a sprint.

Investing vs. Gambling

Both gambling and investing use money to generate more money. Both are high risk. But while investing requires skill, most forms of gambling rely on pure luck.

When you invest in US government bonds or companies like Google and Amazon, you might make or lose some money, but you're highly unlikely to lose all the money you invested. When you gamble on a game or in a casino, it's likely that when you lose, you lose all the money you gambled.

With investing, there are legal protections that ensure that you have as much information as company insiders. With casinos, there's a lot of rigging going on. Some lucky people will win, sure. But most people will lose money, and the house usually wins. In fact, the more you play, the more likely you are to lose.

Saving has little risk, but also low returns. Gambling might be fun, but it's a huge risk. Investing is the perfect middle-ground: you can grow your money at a high rate, but with less risk.

Investing to Reach Your Goals

The secret to investing is buying things that go up in value over time (or that pay you a return for holding them).

When you buy something and its price goes up, you make money. When you buy something and its price goes down, you lose money. (There's also a less common way of making money called "shorting," but we'll talk about this in later lessons.)

The best investors learn what will go up the most in price. They might even figure out the best time to buy them, how much to buy, and when to sell.

We'll cover all of this later. For now, just remember: Investing puts **you** in charge of your money, and not the other way around.

Lesson Four: Why Should I Become an Investor?

There might be a part of you that thinks it's easier to have someone else manage your money for you. But here's the thing: that money manager will charge a fee, and that fee could be as much as 2% every year.

Think about it like this: if you give them $100, they keep $2 and invest the $98 for you.

Now imagine that they charge you $2 every year for 20 years.

Twenty years from now, you would have $60 and they would have $40.

That doesn't sound so bad, does it? But here's the rub: studies have shown that professional money managers don't do a good job at managing your money over time. In fact, they do slightly worse than the average performance of the market.

That's why it's important for YOU to learn how to manage your own money. Knowledge is power. In investing, it can be the difference between making a little and making a lot.

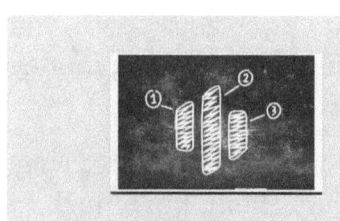

Lesson Five: Learning with Invstr

You're almost done with Module 1! Now's a good time to give you a preview of what's coming in the lessons ahead.

Think of investing knowledge as a set of building blocks: each piece gets you closer to your goal of becoming a skilled investor. When you've mastered the whole thing, you've officially become a boss.

The best investors out there learn the concepts and practice them regularly. Learn at your pace with this book, then put it into practice with a virtual portfolio management game like Invstr's Fantasy Finance.

INVESTING AND YOU

INVESTMENT PRACTICE AND PROCESS

MARKETS AND PEOPLE

BUSINESS AND ECONOMICS

Level 1: Business and Economics

What is a business? How does it make money? How do businesses fit into the economy? How does the economy work and what are its major players? Understanding the structure and operation of a business and the economy is key to becoming a great investor.

This is covered in Modules 2 and 3.

Level 2: Markets and People

Once you have a good understanding of what a business is and how the economy works, you'll start to apply that knowledge to how the economy can impact financial markets, and which factors make them go up or down. You'll also learn about the people who participate in and impact the markets. Because remember: financial markets are all about people. Human decisions, emotions, and psychology play a big role in financial markets (as they do in any marketplace).

This is covered in Modules 4, 5, and 6.

Level 3: Investment Practice and Process

Long-term success doesn't happen just by accident. First, we'll take you through all the things you need to do to get financially fit. Then, we'll help you with your game plan or investment process: you'll need to establish your objectives, develop an investment strategy, create an investment outlook, and choose which investments to make, how much to invest, when to invest, and when to get out.

This is covered in Modules 7 and 8.

Level 4: Investing and You

Once you feel like you have a good understanding of all the key concepts, it's time to take it into the real world and apply your knowledge. You'll learn about how to open a brokerage account. And you'll learn some top tips to help you succeed in the real world.

This is covered in Modules 9 and 10.

Module One Top Tip: What is Interest?

Interest is the cost of borrowing money. Alternatively, it is the fee for lending. It is typically expressed as a percentage of the total borrowed or loan amount.

MODULE TWO

Business Basics

Lesson One: Emma's Lemonade Business – A Case Study

Welcome to Module 2!

We'll be covering some important concepts in the next few lessons. To make them easy to understand, we're gonna use practical examples. So, without further ado, we'd like to introduce you to someone named Emma.

Who is Emma? She's your friend. She also happens to make some *delicious* lemonade.

Emma buys fresh lemons and makes lemonade like a pro. In fact, people love it so much that they're willing to pay money for it.

She decides to take a leap and create a business to start selling her lemonade. And that's where our journey begins...

Lesson Two: Understanding a Business Story

So far, Emma's crushing it. She's got a great recipe for lemonade AND people who want to buy it. That means she has the two ingredients she needs to get her lemonade business going: a product (lemonade) and customers (people who want to buy it).

If Emma were handing out free lemonade, she couldn't call herself a business. As soon as she has a product and people who want to buy it, she becomes a businesswoman.

(FYI: The product doesn't need to be a physical product. It could also be a service like washing cars. Doctors and lawyers also provide services instead of physical products.)

I'm Not A Businessman, I'm A Business, Man.

There are tons of businesses, and they come in all shapes and sizes. Today, most new businesses are digital. They use modern technology as a better way of offering products or services (Amazon, Uber, Netflix).

You can analyze businesses by the:

- Products they offer (do they have one main product or several?)
- Regions they operate in (are they local or global?)

- Clients they serve (individual customers, businesses or governments?)

You can also look at how they offer their services:

- Offline or online
- Single channel or multi-channel (for example, offering products in-store as well as online)

Together, these things tell a business' story. Different businesses have different stories. Some are new, others are old. Some are still growing, while others are stable. Some pay out their profits to their shareholders, others re-invest in the business. Some do not have profits yet. Some are still building their products.

But back to our friend Emma: she sells lemonade to people who love it. The thing that makes her business different is the *quality* of her lemonade.

Understanding the business story is the first part of analyzing a business. Next, let's see how Emma makes her dough.

Lesson Three: Revenues and Net Income

The better Emma's lemonade is, the more money she can charge for it. The money she makes by selling lemonade is called her revenues. Another word for revenues is income - the money that she earns.

Emma's revenues are only half of the story. Let's say her clients pay her $250 in total for the lemonade. Emma first needs to spend money to make the lemonade. That's:

- $100 to buy lemons
- $50 to buy bottles

In total, she spends $150. We call that her costs. Emma's net revenues or profit are the difference between her revenues and her costs:

$250 revenues - $150 costs = $100 net revenues.

Sadly, Emma can't keep all of her net revenues. She needs to pay tax. Cue Imperial Death March...

Corporate Taxes

The government charges businesses tax on their profits. If the business is a company, it pays corporation or corporate tax. In the US, the corporate tax rate is currently 21%. That means that for every $100 of profit a company makes, it needs to pay the US government $21 in tax.

Let's say Emma created a company for her lemonade business. Her company made $100 in net revenues. When we take 21% or $21 away from Emma's net revenues, we get her net income or bottom line.

All of these calculations are published in a company's income statement. Emma's looks like this:

Revenues	+$250
Costs	-$150
Profit	$100
Taxes	-$21
Net Income / Bottom Line	**$79**

In the next lesson, we'll look at the other things we need to understand in Emma's business. Keep going, you're doing great!

Lesson Four: Assets and Liabilities

There are a few things Emma needs before she can get her business going:

- Lemons
- Lemon squeezer
- Lemonade bottles

We call these assets. Assets are items a business owns that it uses to create its products and services. For example: cash, investments, inventory, office equipment, and company-owned vehicles.

But where did Emma get the money to buy her assets? It could've come from one of two main sources:

- Emma borrowed the money from a friend, a family member, or bank.
- Someone (an investor - maybe you?) invested in the business.

Let's check out each option.

Borrowing Money

A business or a company can borrow money to manage and grow its business. This is money that the company has to pay back later.

There's usually a cost to borrowing money. We call this interest. Interest is a percentage of the amount borrowed that the company needs to pay back each year. It's on top of the borrowed amount.

A company can borrow money in two ways:

1. Take out a loan from a bank.
2. Sell bonds. Bonds are loans that can more easily be bought and sold by investors.

Lenders or creditors, the people who lend the money or buy the bonds, are willing to lend money to a business when they believe it can pay them back with interest.

Investors

The second source of money for Emma's business is for her or someone else to invest in her business. An investor is someone who invests in a business. But that doesn't mean they're entitled to get their investment back from the company. Instead, investors usually get:

- The right to vote at company shareholder meetings.
- The right to receive a fair share of any money the company decides to pay back to investors. This money could be in the form of a dividend (a share of the company's profits) or a repayment of other monies (for example, from selling part or all of the business to someone else).

Investor rights are normally specified in the company's Articles of Association and the investors' Share Purchase Agreement.

Some people think that when you buy a share in a business, you're a partial owner of that business. That's kinda misleading. For example, if you bought shares in Starbucks, you can't just walk into a coffee shop and help yourself to a cup of coffee (although that'd be pretty sweet). Really, you only have rights associated with the shares you bought.

If you invest in Emma's business, you can vote for the directors of her business. The directors choose the managers, who run the company on a day-to-day basis. (In our example, the manager would probably be Emma.)

Assets, Liabilities, and Balance Sheets

Both money that's borrowed and investments the company receives are referred to as liabilities. Liabilities are the ways a company funds its assets. Bank debt, mortgage debt, shareholder investments, and taxes owed are all examples of liabilities.

A company's assets and liabilities are detailed on its balance sheet. The reason it's called a balance sheet is because a company's assets always equals its liabilities.

Let's look at what Emma's balance sheet looks like. And let's imagine that both you and Emma invested $100 each in her lemonade business. Emma then puts the money in the bank.

The assets and liabilities of the business would look like this before and after the investments were made:

Before the investments:

ASSETS	LIABILITIES
Cash at bank: $0	Your shares: $0
Emma's shares: $0	
Total Assets: $0	**Total Liabilities: $0**

After the investments:

ASSETS	LIABILITIES
Cash at bank: $200	Your shares: $100
Emma's shares: $100	
Total Assets: $200	**Total Liabilities: $200**

Cash has gone up by $200. This is the money that you both paid in. The liabilities also reflect the $100 that you invested and the $100 that Emma invested.

Now let's imagine that Emma was able to borrow $100 from the local bank. The lemonade business balance sheet would now look like this:

After the $100 borrowing:

ASSETS	LIABILITIES

Cash at bank: $300   Loans from bank: $100
Your shares: $100
Emma's shares: $100
Total Assets: $300   **Total Liabilities: $300**

Cash went up by $100, from $200 to $300. And the loan from the bank was added as a liability. Total assets and liabilities increased from $200 to $300.

Finally, let's add the $79 that Emma's business made in net income.

After the $79 net income:

ASSETS   **LIABILITIES**

Cash at bank: $379   Loans from bank: $100
Your shares: $100
Emma's shares: $100
Total Assets: $379   **Total Liabilities: $379**

Cash went up by $79. The same $79 also shows up as a liability, which is available to be paid out to shareholders as a dividend.

Emma's business is slaying. She's happy, you're happy, birds are singing from the trees. What could go wrong?

Lesson Five: Business Risks

So far, you've learned the basics of what makes a business and a business story. You've learned some important concepts like revenues, costs and net income. You know what's up with assets and liabilities, and how they match on a company's balance sheet. Not bad!

In the final lesson of Module 2, we're gonna look at business risks and where to spot them. Risk is an important part of any business story. You've got to understand risk before you can understand an investment.

Types of Risk:

A risk is something that can go wrong in a business - and believe us, there are tons. Let's go back to our favorite lemonade-maker, Emma.

Clients: Emma's clients could move to another state or decide to drink coconut water instead. This would hurt revenues.

Competitors: Someone else could start making better tasting lemonade. This would hurt the amount of lemonade Emma sells and her revenues.

Product: One of Emma's lemonade bottles could explode. This would freak people out and stop them from buying her lemonade. That would definitely hurt revenues.

Legal: The federal government could make lemonade illegal. This would stop all revenues.

Management: Emma could get the flu and stop making lemonade for a while. This would hurt revenues.

Costs: The price of lemons could go up. This would increase Emma's costs.

Regulatory: The Food & Drug Administration (FDA) could enforce that Emma washes each lemon by hand before she turns it into lemonade. This would increase her costs.

Tax: The government could raise tax on company profits. This would hurt Emma's bottom line or net income.

As an investor, your job is to understand and evaluate the risk of a business. Which risks are specific to a business? Are you getting paid enough to take the risk? Do the potential rewards justify the risks? Do you have too much of the same risk in your investments?

Heads up: you shouldn't always think of risks as bad things. The more risk you're willing to take, the higher return you should expect to earn. Until they go wrong, risks are actually opportunities to make money.

In the broader economy, there are plenty of opportunities to make money and plenty of risks. In the next module, we're gonna leave Emma behind for a while and start looking at the economy as a whole.

You've reached the end of Module 2! Take this virtual high five from me Let's keep going and up your knowledge even more.

Module 2 Top Tip: Single vs. Multi-Channel

A single-channel business is one that sells its product through only one method, or "channel." For example, a local butcher is a single-channel business, because it only sells its products in-store.

A multi-channel business is one that sells its product through multiple different methods, or "channels." For example, Apple is a multi-channel business, because it sells its products both in stores and online.

MODULE THREE

Economics Explained

Lesson One: What is an Economy?

Think of all the businesses you know in your local neighborhood. Now imagine that you could add up the value of all the things those businesses sell. We're talking grocery items, car wash tokens, gas station sales, restaurants, etc.

This is your local economy. It's all of the business activity in a given area.

Our local economy doesn't operate in isolation. There's the regional economy, our national economy, and even the global economy. All of these are important.

The price of a local car wash token might not be too affected by what goes on outside your local economy. But the price of almonds is definitely affected by the weather in California, and the price of gold is affected by the monsoon season in India! And let's not forget that iPhones are made in China.

An economy is a mix of things that happen both locally and more broadly. The process of the world slowly becoming more integrated and us becoming dependent on each other is known as globalization.

Lesson Two: Who are the Main Players in an Economy?

There are three main types of people in an economy. You're already familiar with companies. Companies employ people, invest in land, buildings, machinery, and technology. They buy and sell things.

The people they sell to most are households. Households are families like yours. In most countries, the things they buy and sell make up the largest percentage of the economy.

The third main player is the government. This could be the municipal, state, or federal government. One of the main jobs of a government is to collect taxes. They then spend the money they collect in taxes on things they think are important for us, like school teachers, the fire service, and other community workers.

Together, the things we buy as consumers, the money the government spends, and the investments companies make add up to the national economy.

There's one more thing we need to add to this picture: the amount we trade with people in other countries. We'll look at that in a later lesson!

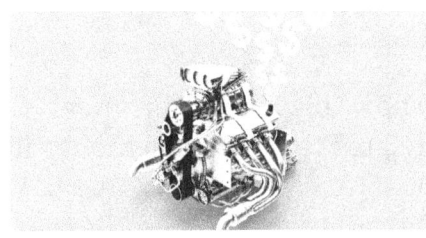

Lesson Three: What Drives an Economy?

Let's focus on the three main players (companies, households, government) and what makes them spend money. Remember, the more money they put into the economy, the more the economy will grow.

Companies

Company investment is driven by two things:

- How confident they feel about their future growth prospects
- How expensive it is for them to borrow and invest

When the economy is strong and borrowing is cheap, companies invest heavily in expanding their business by building new factories, hiring new workers, and researching new technologies.

When the economy is weak and companies are worried that consumers won't buy their products, companies won't expand; they're worried that less revenue in the future might mean that they can't pay back their loans.

Households

Household spending is driven by two things:

- How many people there are in the household
- How much money they have to spend

When wages are increased or taxes are lowered, families will have more money to spend on consumer goods, so household spending increases.

When households have less money to spend - or are saving their money because they're worried about a future downturn - household spending falls.

Governments

Government spending is driven by how "big" the government is, and the size of the government is related to how much money it spends.

A government can spend the money it borrows. It can also spend the money it collects in taxes from households or companies. But a bigger government isn't always good for the economy, especially if high taxes cause households and companies to spend less by the same amount.

To avoid this problem, governments borrow money and spend that instead, knowing that they'll have to pay it back eventually. Governments have to make sure they spend money that will make the economy bigger and generate enough additional tax revenues in the future to pay back what they borrowed.

Lesson Four: What is Trade?

We live in a municipality, which is part of a district, which is part of a state, which is part of a country, which is part of the world.

Still with me?

International Trade and Trade Balance

International trade is becoming more and more important to

the global economy. It's a key reason why we've grown over the past twenty years!

What do I mean by trade? Let's look at an example:

If the US sells $100 million of Boeing planes to China, this **adds** to the size of the US economy. The US has generated an additional $100mm of revenues from China.

If the US buys $100mm of toys from China, this **reduces** the size of the US economy. The US spent money abroad that it could have spent at home.

The difference between what we export (e.g. Boeings) and what we import (e.g. Chinese toys) is called the trade balance.

A positive trade balance means that we export more than we import, which makes our economy larger.

A negative trade balance means we export less than we import, which makes our economy smaller.

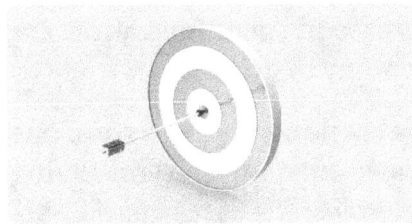

Lesson Five: Why Do We Trade?

Remember your friend Emma? Let's go back to her for a second...

Emma isn't just a talented lemonade maker. She also makes great bread. In fact, she could spend less time making lemonade and more time making bread. However, Emma is not as good at making bread as the local baker, so she sticks to making lemonade. She uses the money she makes from her lemonade to buy bread from the baker.

Emma now has lemonade to drink and sell, and bread to eat. She's better off than if she made her own bread and lemonade.

The same principle applies internationally. Trade allows us to concentrate on the things we're good at and exchange them with other countries. The more we focus on what we do well, the better off we all are, and the more the global economy grows.

For example, the Chinese economy grew rapidly after establishing trade deals with countries worldwide, such as the US. China, which has plenty of labor and factories, sent over cheap manufactured goods to the US. In return, the US sent back more advanced goods like cars and computers.

What was the result? The Chinese economy gained access to advanced technologies, while manufactured goods like clothes and toys became much cheaper in the US. Both countries got huge benefits from trade!

Lesson Six: What is Growth?

The economy is made up of all of the spending in an area. An increase in spending causes the economy to grow.

Growth is the amount the size of the economy changes from one quarter to the next. Growth can be awesome for everyone living in an economy. When an economy grows, the stock market becomes stronger, new technology and products become available, and people tend to be well off.

For this reason, economies normally want stable growth over time. That's why politicians and the media focus so much on the growth of an economy.

It's also why they try so hard to avoid the wrong side of growth: recession. Recession is when the economy shrinks for two or more quarters in a row.

We've felt the effects of recessions before. The 2008 Great Recession was one of the worst periods for the world economy since World War II, and left people, companies, and countries all struggling to afford necessities and unable to pay back debts. It's events like these that remind us just why governments and central banks work so hard to avoid recessions, and to minimize their negative effects when they do happen.

Growth is awesome. Recessions are not. Our collective ability to extend growth for as long as possible is called the economic cycle. We'll look at this soon, but first, we need to talk about the economy's main potential enemy...

Lesson Seven: What is Inflation?

Let's go back to Emma. She sells her lemonade for $1 per bottle. Her clients love her lemonade so much that they're willing to keep buying her lemonade, even if she increases the price from $1.00 to $1.10 per bottle.

Because Emma is only a small producer of lemonade, the price change has a relatively small impact on her clients, and even less on the economy as a whole.

Now imagine that it's not just the price of Emma's lemonade that increases, but the price of everything that people consume in the economy. This is called a rise in inflation.

How does this impact the economy as a whole?

First, anyone who has money in the bank or a fixed salary will realize that they can't buy as much with their dollars as before. This is called a reduction in purchasing power. It impacts all of our three main players: households, governments, and companies.

If people think prices will continue rising, their behavior will start to change. They'll buy goods now, instead of waiting for the future. Companies do the same.

This acceleration in economic activity can get out of hand. At an extreme, it leads to shortages of goods in shops, because people buy and hoard goods they don't need.

The economy could also get to a point where it's unable to produce more goods. At this point, inflation could start to accelerate even more. When inflation is extremely high and accelerating, it's called hyper-inflation.

Once our goods are priced higher than other countries, they also become less competitive internationally. This worsens the trade balance, and can lead to exporters going out of business and people losing their jobs.

To prevent things from getting out of control, central banks like the Federal Reserve raise interest rates. This makes it more expensive to take out a loan, which impacts anyone who has borrowed or needs to borrow money, like households with mortgages, companies who borrow to invest, and the cost of government borrowing. As interest rates continue to rise, people start spending less and the economy slows down. Company profits fall, as does the stock market.

It's a cycle of ups and downs, and it can be a little confusing! Let's investigate more in the next section…

Lesson Eight: What is the Economic Cycle?

As you know, there are tons of things going on in the economy. Our behavior is impacted by our expectations about the future as well as political events at home and abroad.

The Economic Cycle

Client demand, production costs, and interest rates can all impact a single business or an entire economy. Generally, we become overly optimistic at the top of the economic cycle and overly-pessimistic at the bottom.

Central banks try to stop us from getting overly-optimistic by raising interest rates. Governments try to stop us from getting overly-pessimistic by spending money to support the economy.

We've all seen the economic cycle in action. After the 2001 recession, goods became cheaper, companies invested heavily, and many people bought homes using loans.

Then, in 2007, after years of heavy spending and growth, everything crashed: people and companies went bankrupt when they couldn't pay back their debts, and the economy fell to record lows. In the years after, the economy recovered and enjoyed steady growth, with US stock markets hitting record highs in 2019.

The Economic Cycle in Action: An Example

For now, let's just imagine that the entire economy consists of Emma, her clients, and a bank. One day, a client buys more lemonade than normal from Emma. She gets excited and decides to produce and sell more lemonade. She goes to her bank and borrows money to buy more lemons and bottles. She also decides to hire her brother's friend to deliver the lemonade.

The plan works: Emma is able to sell more lemonade. She goes back to the bank to borrow more money. She hires another delivery driver. Her business is growing.

At some point, Emma is unable to buy more lemons and bottles, which means she's also unable to sell all the lemonade her clients want. Her clients are disappointed and decide to start drinking water instead.

Things get worse: the bank manager asks Emma to pay him more for the money she borrowed. To pay the bank, she is forced to fire one of her delivery drivers. Because her business is not as strong as it was before, she decides to fire her brother's friend and reduce the price of her lemonade.

In time, the bank decides that it can charge Emma less to borrow money. Her clients think that her lemonade is cheap again and decide to buy more. Emma begins to have more confidence to invest in her business once again....

The economy is cyclical, and we must learn to ride the highs and minimize losses during the lows.

The economic cycle has a direct impact on financial markets. In the next module, we'll take a look at these markets and what makes them go up and down!

Module 3 Top Tip: The Trade Balance

Trade balance is the difference between a country's exports and imports. If a country exports more than it imports, it has a *positive* trade balance; if a country imports more than it exports, it has a *negative* trade balance

MODULE FOUR

Market Magic

Lesson One: Prices and Financial Markets

You've made it to Module 4! Give yourself a high five. Now, we're getting to the good stuff.

In Module 3, we learned about the economy. Remember, the economy is the sum of all the economic activities of businesses, people, and government. The economy also includes our trade with other countries. The more we produce, consume, and trade, the bigger our economy.

In this module, we'll learn how the economy impacts financial markets and what makes the price of financial products go up or down.

Exchanges

Our economy is based on an exchange of goods. Let's go back to your friend Emma. If she wants to buy a car, she needs to give the car dealer something in return - he wouldn't give his cars away for free! Emma could give the car dealer her lemonade in exchange. But it would take a huge amount of lemonade, not to mention how hard it would be for Emma to transport it all. Plus, the car dealer probably doesn't even want all that lemonade.

This is why we use money instead in our economy. Money is easier to exchange, and the car dealer can now buy whatever he wants.

Market Price and Market Economy

Everything in the economy has a monetary value (the dollar price at which people are willing to buy or sell something). The price of Emma's lemonade bottles depends on what she wants to sell it for and what someone is willing to pay for it.

No one will buy Emma's lemonade if the price she charges is too high. However, Emma will not want to sell her lemonade if her clients only want to buy the lemonade at a very low price.

As a result, the market price of every good or service is the price at which both the buyer and the seller are happy. The market price is based on both supply and demand.

If more people demand lemons, the sellers are able to charge more for their lemons because people are willing to pay a higher price for lemons. The market price goes up.

If people don't want lemons, the sellers won't be able to charge very much for their lemons. The market price goes down.

This kind of an economy is called a market economy. Prices in a market economy are set by buyers and sellers. Prices go up when demand increases or supply decreases. Prices go down when demand decreases or when supply increases.

An Example: The Farmer's Market

If prices are set by buyers and sellers, why is it that the same good sells for the same price across a market? Why do cans of Coke sell for the exact same price in every store in New York City?

Let's imagine a farmer's market, where there are multiple stands selling lemons. If one of the stands is selling lemons for $0.50 and all the other stands are selling lemons for $1.00, then everyone will want to buy lemons from the $0.50 stand. The other lemon stands will be run out of business - no one wants to buy their lemons when another stand in the market is selling the same thing for half the price!

The same is true for all the other things in the market. As people buy and sell food items, the price of each food will become more consistent as buyers seek out the cheapest option. The more expensive sellers will be forced to adjust. Eventually, there will be a single price for the same food.

The rest of the economy sets its prices in the same way, especially because it's become easier for us to compare prices from different sellers, thanks to online shopping and the digital marketplace.

The financial world works similarly. The price of different financial products is set by financial markets. These are the places where the price of financial products is determined, just as the price of lemons is determined in a food market.

In the rest of Module 4, we're going to look at all the major financial markets and understand what they are and what makes their price go up or down. Understanding this is a huge part of becoming a successful investor!

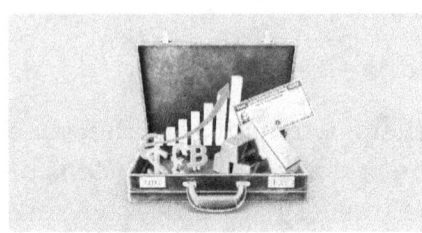

Lesson Two: What are Asset Classes?

In the financial world, there are different categories and subcategories of financial products, all with different behaviors and reasons for why their prices move up and down.

In this module, we'll learn why.

Asset Classes

Let's start by understanding the different categories of financial products. Financial categories are called asset classes. The main asset classes are:

1. Currencies
2. Bonds
3. Equities
4. Commodities
5. Cryptocurrencies

There are *many* other asset classes, like real estate, private equity, even wine and classic cars! In this book, we're going to focus on the main ones you're more likely to buy or sell.

Why Use Asset Classes?

Asset classes help us group together financial products that have similar behaviors. Their prices rise and fall together because those prices are determined by similar economic factors and world trends.

For example: when a government announces a new tax on

banks, financial company stocks (which are part of the *equities* asset class) will fall in price at the same time, but the other asset classes will remain relatively unaffected.

As investors, we use asset classes to decide *how* to build our investment portfolios. By investing in many different asset classes, we create a diverse portfolio that ensures individual shocks and events don't cost us too much.

For example: if the equities asset class falls sharply, investors with only equities in their portfolios will lose more money than investors with equities, bonds, and commodities all in their portfolio. (You'll learn more about portfolio building and diversification in Module 8.)

In the rest of this module, we'll learn about the main asset classes, how they behave, and what makes their prices go up or down.

Lesson Three: What are Currencies and Foreign Exchanges?

The simplest asset class to understand is currencies. Think of the money in your pocket or bank account. If you're in the US, this is probably the US dollar.

The US dollar is a currency. It's money issued by the US government and used by people in the United States to buy and sell different products and services. The currency of a country is sometimes also referred to as the legal tender of a country.

Sharing a Currency

Some countries share the same currency. They don't have their own unique currency, but use either someone else's currency or a common currency. Several countries, like Ecuador, use the

US dollar as their national currency. Their economies are either too small to justify having their own currency, or are so closely linked to the United States that it makes sense to use the US dollar.

In Europe, countries within the Eurozone all use the Euro instead of a national currency. That means that if a Frenchman goes to Germany, he can use the same currency in both countries.

Other countries don't share the same currency, but base their currency's value on the value of another. For example, Panama's currency, the balboa, is pegged directly to the US dollar at a one-to-one conversion. What this means: although Panama has a different currency from the US, balboas can always be swapped directly for the same amount in US dollars, and will have the exact same value.

Foreign Exchange

Countries that don't share the same currency must exchange their own currency for the foreign one. So, if our girl Emma wanted to buy lemons in the UK, she would need to exchange US dollars for British pounds.

These kinds of transactions are called foreign exchange. The foreign exchange rate is the price relationship between two currencies.

In the past, most world currencies were based on how much gold those currencies could buy. Because of this, foreign exchange was based on the gold standard - to exchange currency, you would receive the amount of the other currency that could buy as much gold as your original currency. For example: if a gold bar cost 100 dollars but only 75 pounds, you could swap 100 dollars for 75 pounds.

Today, we don't base currency prices on gold, but on market price.

Flat Currencies

Currencies that aren't based on anything are known as fiat currencies. Fiat currencies go up and down in value based on how much of each currency the market demands. Just like the lemons in the lemon market.

The Foreign Exchange Rate

Now let's look at how foreign exchange works. The foreign exchange rate between the US dollar and the British pound is called GBPUSD.

- The first currency is called the base currency.
- The second currency is called the quoted currency.

So, for this example, "GBP" refers to the Great British pound and "USD" to the US dollar.

Let's say that the price of GBPUSD, or the foreign exchange rate, is 1.25. That means that one British pound is worth 1.25 US dollars. If your friend Emma needed to buy British pounds, she would have to exchange 1.25 USD for every GBP she wanted to buy.

If you wanted to invest in the British pound, you would buy pounds hoping that the foreign exchange rate would rise. That would mean that each British pound you bought would be worth more USD than the 1.25 dollars you bought them for.

In the next lesson, we'll look at what makes the foreign exchange rate go up or down. Stay with it! You're doing great.

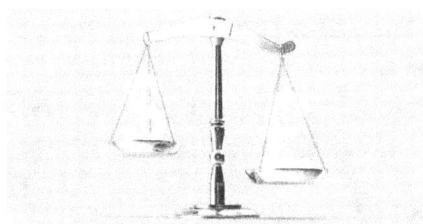

Lesson Four: What Makes Foreign Exchange Rates Go Up and Down?

Earlier, we learned that demand

for a good or service pushes the price up, while supply of a good or service pushes the price down. The market price of a good is the point at which supply and demand are in balance.

The foreign exchange rate is the price of one currency against another. So, what are the factors that might increase the supply or demand of one currency relative to another?

We use foreign exchange to make financial transactions in other countries. As a result, a currency's foreign exchange rate is determined by the number of people who want to make transactions in that currency.

Sound complicated? I promise it's not! Let's walk through an example...

Imagine that your friend Emma learned that British lemons are cheaper than American ones. She would stop buying her lemons in the US and instead buy them from the UK using British pounds.

To do this, Emma must buy GBP with her USD, which increases the demand for GBP. Since the demand for GBP has increased, sellers can charge more USD per GBP, causing the GBPUSD exchange rate to increase.

The cycle of a currency's changing supply and demand is how an exchange rate rises and falls.

Now, let's look at five variables that change a currency's foreign exchange rate.

Variable 1: Exports are good for a currency

Let's say Emma is importing lemons from the UK into the US. She needs to buy GBP to buy the lemons, increasing demand for GBP. This increase in demand allows sellers to charge more USD for GBP, causing the GBPUSD exchange rate to go up.

Variable 2: High inflation is bad for a currency

Remember, inflation is an increase in prices within an economy. The price of a country's goods influences trade.

Let's say Emma was buying lemons from the UK because they were only £0.40 ($0.50), but US lemons were $1.00 each. If Emma's British lemons went up in price from £0.40 to £1.00 ($1.25), Emma would stop buying British lemons. She would buy them in the US instead, because American lemons are only $1.

If all UK goods became more expensive relative to US goods, Americans would buy fewer UK goods, and more US goods. The demand for GBP would then decrease, causing the GBPUSD exchange rate to go down.

Variable 3: A strong economy is good for the currency

When a country is doing well economically, it attracts foreign investment. So, when foreigners see how well Emma's lemonade business is doing, they might decide that they also want to open businesses in the US, or they might expand their current businesses in the US.

We call foreign money coming into a country capital inflow. These inflows increase the demand for a currency and push up its exchange rate.

Variable 4: High interest rates are good for a currency

When interest rates in a country are high, investors from abroad want to gain from the high interest rates. They do this by depositing money in that country's banks or buying that country's bonds, because the returns on their investment are higher than at home.

To do so, they must buy that country's currency. This increased demand for a currency will result in an increase in the price of that currency, driving up the foreign exchange rate.

Variable 5: Stable politics are good for a currency

When a country has a strong and stable government, more people are likely to bring their money there from abroad. This is also good for a currency. Conversely, when people are worried about the political situation, they send their money abroad for safety.

Lesson Five: What are Bonds?

In Module 2, we saw Emma borrowing money from the bank to grow her business. Another way for her to borrow money is to sell bonds.

A bond is like an IOU (I-owe-you). It's a contract between the borrower (Emma) and the lender (the person who buys the bond). The people buying the bonds are essentially lending money to Emma.

For example, if Emma sells a $100 bond to a lender, she'll be able to spend that $100 now, which she'll pay back to the lender later. The difference between a bond and a loan is that if a bond owner needs her money back, she can sell the bond to someone else.

At a certain date, the bond expires and Emma must repay whoever is holding the bond on that date, along with the interest the bond has accumulated. In this way, a bond is essentially a loan that can be traded between people.

Lots of people within an economy borrow money through bonds. The government uses bonds to borrow money for the federal budget. States and municipalities use bonds. Companies use bonds.

Selling a bond to borrow money is called issuing a bond. It becomes a liability for the entity issuing it.

Bonds come in all shapes and sizes, but they usually have some common features:

- Principal amount or Issue size: the amount that the borrower or issuer needs to pay back.
- Maturity: the date the issuer needs to pay back the bond. The longer the maturity date, the riskier the bond typically is. A few bonds have no maturity date. The borrower never has to repay the principal, but has to keep on paying the interest rate forever! These bonds are referred to as perpetuals.
- Coupon: the interest rate the borrower has agreed to pay to the bondholders. Interest rates are usually fixed. This is why bonds are sometimes referred to as fixed income. The borrower pays the same interest rate every six months until maturity. Sometimes, the interest rate varies and is reset every three or six months. These bonds are called floating rate notes.

After a bond has been issued, it's bought and sold between banks or through electronic marketplaces. Investors like to buy bonds because they can estimate with greater certainty the returns they'll get by holding a bond to maturity.

In the next lesson, we'll look at the factors that change the price of a bond!

Lesson Six: What Makes Bond Prices Go Up and Down?

Let's imagine that we want to buy $100 worth of Emma's lemonade bonds. In this scenario:

- The maturity of the bond (the date when she'll pay us back our money) is six months.
- The coupon or interest rate she's paying is 10%.
- The price we pay for the bond is 100% of $100. (When the price is set at 100%, we also call this par.)

What could affect the price of Emma's lemonade bond?

Variable 1: Better credit quality increases the price of the bond

The first is the likelihood that Emma will pay us back our money. When we buy a bond at par, we expect to receive all of this money back after the bond matures.

However, if there's a risk that Emma won't be able to pay us back the full amount, we want to pay less than par. Instead, we'd rather pay $90 in the hopes that we'll receive $100 at maturity, because we're worried about the risk of not receiving anything at all.

But if we're certain Emma can pay us back, we pay more than par; we're happy to pay $105 to receive $100 at maturity, because we know that we'll receive that entire $100, along with the interest she's paying. This means we're confident about receiving $110 from a $105 investment.

Because of this, we have to look at how likely it is that Emma pays us back. This is called the credit quality of the issuer. If Emma's business booms, she'll be making a lot of money, and she'll also be more likely to pay us back, resulting in bond prices rising above par.

If Emma's business worsens and it seems unlikely that she'll have enough money to pay us back, bond prices will fall below par, and buying her bonds becomes riskier.

Variable 2: Lower market interest rates increase the price of the bond

The second consideration that affects bond prices is the level of interest rates. Imagine this: after Emma issues her bonds with a 10% coupon, other businesses with similar credit quality start selling $100 bonds with coupons of only 8%. Investors will realize that even though Emma and her competitors are just as likely to pay back the $100 of principal, Emma's bonds pay out more interest than the rest of the market. This makes investors want to buy Emma's bonds more, because they'll receive more money by holding Emma's bonds instead of other ones. Since they'll receive more money from Emma's bonds, investors are happy to pay more for Emma's bonds, which increases the price of Emma's bonds.

However, if interest rates rise, and Emma's competitors all sell bonds with 12% coupons, investors will know that Emma's 10% coupon bonds don't pay as much as her competitors. The price investors are willing to pay for her bonds will fall.

Overall, bond prices go up when interest rates fall, but bond prices fall when interest rates go up.

Lesson Seven: What are Equities?

In Module 2, we saw Emma put $100 of her own money into her lemonade business. YOU also put in $100 into her business. This money is known as equity, and is represented by shares. These shares are contracts that represent a fraction of ownership of that company.

Shareholders

The people who put capital into a business are called shareholders. Shareholders' names are entered into a shareholder register maintained by the company's registrar.

Shareholders have the right to:

- Vote at company shareholder meetings, including the Annual General Meeting. Here, they vote for the Directors of the company. Directors choose the managers, who run the company on a day-to-day basis.
- Receive a fair share of any money the company pays back to investors. This money could be in the form of a dividend (a share of the company's profits) or a repayment of other monies (for example, from selling part or all of the business to someone else).

Going Public

There are millions of companies in the world. Most of them are private companies. Their shares are not publicly available for other people to buy or sell.

When companies want to let public investors buy or sell their equity to raise even more money, they list the company on one or more stock exchanges, the marketplace for equities. They might also offer shares in the company for sale to the public. If they're raising fresh capital, it's called an Initial Public Offering or IPO. The capital raised in an IPO is re-invested into the company.

Trading

Shares in a company can also be traded between investors. After an investor buys shares directly from the company on the primary market, he or she can then sell those shares to other investors on the secondary market. When the shares are sold, the new owner of the shares receives all of the shareholder's rights that the shares entail. However, the money this investor spent on these shares only goes to the seller who sold the shares - not the company itself.

Stock Exchanges

There are many different stock exchanges around the world. In the US alone, there are over 10 stock exchanges! You've probably heard of the New York Stock Exchange (NYSE) and National Association of Securities Dealers Automated Quotations (NASDAQ).

Stock exchanges open at certain hours of the day, usually from Monday to Friday. They're carefully regulated to make sure all investors are treated fairly. For example, there are restrictions on when company insiders can buy or sell shares and how company news is reported to the public.

Don't stop now, you're more than halfway done with this module! Onward.

Lesson Eight: What Makes Equity Prices Go Up and Down?

Let's imagine that Emma's lemonade business got listed on the NYSE. Awesome, right? Why would the price of her company's shares move up or down? There are a few variables at play...

Variable 1: Revenues and profits affect a company's share price

If Emma is able to grow her business by selling more lemonade, other investors will want to buy shares in her company.

The more profits Emma is able to produce, the more cash she has in the bank and the larger her assets. The bigger Emma's assets, the more valuable the equity of the shareholders and the price per share of the company.

Variable 2: Changes in the level of dividends can affect a company's share price

If Emma's business is making so much money that she's able to share more of her profits via dividends, investors who like to invest for income (such as a pension fund) will buy more of her shares. This increase in demand will push up the price of her shares.

Variable 3: The quality of leadership or management at a company affects a company's share price

Emma has built a successful business and her shareholders believe in her. If Emma is able to recruit great managers to help her grow the business, other shareholders would be willing to pay more for Emma's shares, as they believe this team will grow the business and make it more successful.

If something bad happened to Emma, they might worry that the business would not do so well going forward, causing investors to sell their shares, which would push the price down.

Variable 4: Analyst recommendations impact sentiment for a company's share price.

Many large public companies have multiple independent research analysts carefully following all the news of the companies' performance. They publish research reports indicating whether investors should BUY, HOLD, or SELL their shares.

These research reports can be influential in driving the price of a company's shares up or down, as investors will often make decisions based on analyst recommendations.

Variable 5: Legal, regulatory, and tax changes can push a share price up or down

All companies are subject to laws and regulations that ensure fairness for businesses and consumers. New laws, regulations, and taxes can impact how much money a company will make, moving the share price up or down.

Variable 6: Labor, commodity, and interest costs can affect a company's share price

All companies have costs. Some of the biggest costs are labor costs, raw materials, and interest rates on money they borrow. Lower costs will help a company's profits rise. Higher costs will affect business margins and cause profits to fall.

For example: news that the workers in a company's factory are going on strike could reduce revenues, decreasing both the company's value and its paid dividends, which will drive the price of a share down.

Variable 7: Mergers and acquisitions can cause a company's share price to rise or fall

A popular way for a company to grow is through buying other companies. Sometimes, it's easier to let someone else build a business and then buy that business, rather than trying to build a business yourself.

For example: other drinks companies might not have Emma's lemonade expertise, but they have customers who want to buy lemonade. They might decide to buy Emma's business and sell more of her lemonade to their other customers. They buy the business by buying up all of its issued shares.

But if Emma and her other shareholders don't want to part with her business, they'll demand the buyer pay a premium on top of the current market price for their shares. This premium could be 30% or more. This will cause the price of Emma's shares to increase, as investors will know that they'll be paid a premium price on the share if the sale goes through.

However, this sale might be off-putting to the shareholders of the acquiring business, who don't want to pay such a big premium for Emma's lemonade business - especially if they have to borrow more money to pay for it. It's common for the acquirer's share price to fall upon announcing its intention to acquire another company.

There are many variables that impact the price of a company's shares. As a budding investor, it's important to read the news and understand a company's performance in order to make informed decisions.

Lesson Nine: What are Commodities?

Commodities are a type of asset class. They're traded on different exchanges like NYMEX (New York Mercantile Exchange) and CME (Chicago Mercantile Exchange).

Within commodities, there are four main sub-asset classes:

1. Crude oil: Crude oil consists of the unrefined oil drilled for around the world. It's then sold to refineries and gas distributors. Crude oil gets its value from the global demand for gas and petroleum products; since oil refiners make their profits from selling refined petroleum products, they demand crude oil that they'll then process and distribute.
2. Power and Natural Gas: Power is the electricity that's produced by power plants. Many of these use natural gas to drive their turbines. Natural gas is often found in large gas deposits close to oil deposits. It is piped in large pipelines or liquefied and shipped in special ships to gas terminals around the world.
3. Precious and base metals: Precious metals, like gold and platinum, and base metals, like copper and aluminum, are mined from the earth and refined. Each metal derives its value from its usage in technology and

manufacturing - such as gold in computer CPUs and copper in electrical wires - and its rarity.

4. Agricultural products: are the raw foods that we grow and breed, including everything from corn to coffee to pork bellies. These goods derive their value from human demand for these agricultural products to stock supermarkets, feed farm animals, and to use these natural products to make other goods.

Complications

There's a big difference between commodities and all of the other asset classes we've been discussing. Unlike currencies, bonds, and equities, commodities are physical, not digital. This brings up complications that don't exist with the other asset classes!

One complication is storage. When you buy a bond, currency or equity, a record of your ownership is usually held digitally on a computer somewhere.

However, commodities can't be stored digitally. Take oil, for example. We produce and consume 100 million barrels of oil every day. Oil needs to be transported and stored in a special, environmentally safe facility. All of these things - producing, transporting, refining, and distributing - cost money.

Another complication is weather. Because commodities are physical and mined from the earth, grown, or bred, weather conditions can affect both the demand and supply of commodities, unlike digital financial assets.

We'll see how all of these things impact the price of commodities in the next lesson!

Lesson Ten: What Makes Commodity Prices Go Up and Down?

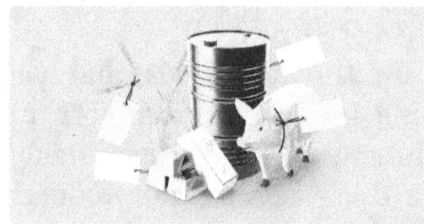Commodities can be difficult to store and expensive to transport by road, rail, or sea. The cost of storage and transportation means that businesses like to hold as little of a commodity as possible. As a result, a small change in demand or supply can have a big impact on the price of a commodity.

This makes commodities riskier than some other asset classes, because the price can move up and down sharply and suddenly. We call movement of prices volatility.

What are the variables that can move a commodity's price up or down?

Variable 1: Political tensions

Many commodities are produced in unstable parts of the world. For example, most of the world's oil is produced in the Middle East. Thirty-five percent of all oil shipped around the world passes through the Straits of Hormuz, a narrow strip of water separating Iran and Arab states. Political risk and war in emerging countries can impact the supply of commodities, pushing up the price of a commodity when supplying it becomes more expensive and riskier.

Variable 2: Economic growth

As the economy grows, we build more houses, offices, cars, and ships. We fly more, drive more, and consume more food. Everything in the economy uses commodities, whether it's energy or materials. The more the economy expands, the greater the demand for commodities. Higher demand pushes commodity prices up.

Variable 3: Inventory levels

Inventories are backup storages that companies and governments keep to avoid running out of necessary commodities in times of high demand or low supply. Investors carefully monitor changes in inventory levels to assess how quickly the price might react if demand or supply changes.

If inventory levels are high, the owners of the inventory can sell them when demand increases. This can prevent the price of the commodity from rising too much. But if inventories are low and demand increases, there is less available spare capacity to meet the increased demand. So, the price of commodities is more likely to rise.

Variable 4: Weather

The weather impacts commodities in two ways. Bad weather or droughts can impact the supply of agricultural products, ruining crops and decreasing supply. Good weather can produce bumper harvests, creating more crops than usual and increasing supply. Heat or cold also affect the demand for energy to heat or cool our homes - prices for home heating or cooling rise during extreme weather events!

Variable 5: US dollar

Many, if not most, commodities are priced in US dollars. That means that when people want to buy commodities, they need to buy US dollars first.

If the US dollar is expensive relative to their own currency, commodity producers will increase their commodity's supply to earn more dollars and even more local currency. Meanwhile, commodity consumers and investors tend to buy fewer commodities if the US dollar is expensive relative to their own currency.

The combination of more supply and less demand results in prices falling, because many suppliers will have to fight to give the lowest price to the relatively few buyers.

The opposite happens when the US dollar is cheap, resulting in high demand and low supply. This allows suppliers to increase prices.

Overall, the price of commodities tends to fall when the US dollar is expensive and rise when the US dollar is cheap.

Lesson Eleven: What are Cryptocurrencies?

Cryptocurrencies are digital tokens that can be exchanged between people electronically. But how and why did they get created? Let's take a quick step into the past...

After the financial crisis of 2008, many people lost faith in the financial system. They were afraid that central banks were "printing" too much money and that this would devalue the national currency.

To counter this, they started to devise an alternative to money that wouldn't be controlled by central banks.

Bitcoin

Bitcoin was the first of these alternatives to become highly popular. Bitcoin has two important properties:

1. The amount of Bitcoin that's created is predetermined. Because the supply of Bitcoin has been fixed in advance by complex rules, it cannot be interfered with.
2. When people exchange Bitcoin with each other, this exchange is agreed by everyone in the Bitcoin system. The terms of their deal are called a smart contract. The smart contract describes the agreement that the two parties have reached.

Verification

Other people in the Bitcoin system help these two parties to complete their agreement. They verify that the seller really has the Bitcoin he or she claims to have. They also agree that the buyer has the means to pay for the Bitcoin they wish to purchase or has fulfilled the terms of the smart contract.

The Blockchain

Once this is verified, the exchange between the buyer and seller is recorded on a public database. This public database is called a blockchain. This record cannot be changed. It forms an immutable part of the "chain" on the blockchain.

The exact identity of the buyers and sellers on the blockchain is kept private. Each buyer or seller has a public key, a special code that identifies them. They also have a private key that unlocks access to their digital wallet where they store their Bitcoin or other cryptocurrencies. Think of it like a super complex PIN code that cannot be easily hacked.

The advantage of the Bitcoin blockchain is that any two people anywhere in the world can exchange Bitcoin tokens with each other without having to know or trust each other. The system verifies their ability to exchange the tokens and it then records the exchange publicly so that neither side can pull out.

The potential benefits of this are enormous: any two people could trade with each other with the confidence that they won't be cheated by the other person. It could lead to a huge increase in direct "trade" between people boosting the global economy.

Why Cryptos?

Philosophically, the strongest supporters of cryptocurrencies see them as a reaction against what they perceive as corrupt financial systems. Governments around the world have borrowed and spent money rather than investing in the future.

Central banks have accommodated this "irresponsible" behavior by printing more fiat currency to buy government bonds and paper over the underlying weakness of the economy. Cryptocurrency enthusiasts want to create a system which is immune to the meddling of politicians and central bankers. It's a highly reactionary political philosophy.

Economically, blockchain, the technology underlying all cryptocurrencies promises great rewards. Since Adam Smith first wrote the Wealth of Nations in 1776, we've understood that trade between nations improves economic wellbeing. Blockchain makes it theoretically possible for any two individuals anywhere in the world to trade with each other without needing to know each other or trust each other. Once a reality, this would help to unlock the full potential of mankind and bring great wealth and prosperity to the planet.

Challenges

Despite the perceived benefits, blockchain and cryptocurrencies do face some challenges:

1. Security: there have been numerous instances of cryptocurrencies being hacked and stolen. Billions of US dollars' worth of crypto currencies have been stolen by computer hackers.
2. Scalability: blockchain suffers from lack of scalability. The Bitcoin protocol is only able to process 7 transactions per second, which is far too low to become commercially useful. By contrast, Visa and Mastercard can process 40,000 transactions per second!
3. Custody: people need to manage their store of cryptocurrencies themselves, instead of relying on a centralized guardian of their assets like a bank. Cryptocurrencies are decentralized by their nature.
4. Ease of buying: buying cryptocurrencies has not been easy. Many banks have been reluctant to allow custom-

ers to use their bank accounts to buy cryptocurrencies with US dollars.
5. Regulation: regulators have also started to crack down on many of the cryptocurrencies, claiming that they breach security laws.

Ultimately, there are many problems to solve before cryptocurrencies and blockchains are able to unlock the potential benefits they offer. This hasn't stopped a huge number of other cryptocurrencies from being created. Some claim to be faster than Bitcoin. Some have different ways of verifying the exchanges or transactions recorded on the blockchain.

Despite this, cryptocurrencies have proved popular, especially with younger generations. This is a new asset class that has made many people very rich very quickly. It's an asset class that isn't dominated by the traditional money managers who have pushed up the price of real estate, equities, and bonds over the last thirty years. Younger people feel they can understand it better than older generations.

In the next lesson, we'll look at what drives the price of cryptocurrencies. Hang in there, you're almost finished!

Twelve: What Makes Cryptocurrency Prices Go Up and Down?

It'd be amazing if we could all use cryptocurrencies safely to trade with each other around the world, right? If that were to happen, the value and (therefore the price) of cryptocurrencies would rise. Like any other fiat currency, cryptocurrencies rely on their broad acceptance as a means of exchange in the new digital world, not on any intrinsic value like bonds or equities.

The main influence on the price of cryptocurrencies is the progress that we make towards that vision. Prices rise when people believe that cryptocurrencies are going to be widely adopted. They fall when prospects look more uncertain.

That confidence or uncertainty is determined by a number of variables:

Variable 1: Security

Greater security of cryptocurrency wallets and transactions is good for crypto prices. Any time that security is shaken (like when a major store of cryptos is hacked and robbed) the price drops. This is because investors want to know that their investments will stay in their hands - not get stolen by hackers.

Variable 2: Scalability

If a cryptocurrency can be exchanged quicker, it can be used for more transactions, causing overall demand for that currency to increase as the number of transactions using that cryptocurrency increases.

Variable 3: Mining Costs

In the blockchain system, the people who verify the transactions and record them to the blockchain are called miners. They're rewarded for their efforts with crypto tokens. The more expensive it is for miners to do their work - mainly electricity to power their computers - the more value they expect in return for their tokens.

Variable 4: Adoption

A few retailers have started to accept cryptos in addition to US dollars and other fiat currencies. The more people who are happy to be paid in crypto, the more valuable it becomes as a form of money.

Variable 5: Liquidity

As more people buy and sell cryptos, the total volume of trades increases, and the ease of buying or selling at any given price also increases. This encourages more people to buy and sell, and also increases the value of cryptos.

Variable 6: Volatility

The flip side of liquidity is volatility: the amount by which the price moves up and down. If there are wild swings in price, cryptos become less useful as a means of exchange. They also become more dangerous as an investment, decreasing the number of investors seeking to buy this cryptocurrency. Ultimately, greater price volatility is bad for the price level of cryptocurrencies.

Variable 7: Regulators

Regulators like central banks and security regulators want to prevent abuse of the financial system. They also want to prevent consumers from being defrauded by illegitimate crypto projects. Some regulators, like those in India and China, have banned the use of crypto altogether.

The more regulators restrict the use of cryptos, the more negative it is for prices. Once they become comfortable with the use of cryptos within the economy, we could expect to see cryptos appreciate in price.

Lesson Thirteen: A Word on Derivatives and Other Financial Products

You might have heard of futures, options, and other products like forwards, swaps, structured notes, CDOs, and more. These financial products are known as derivatives. They're creative but complicated methods financial engineers have developed to buy and sell different asset classes.

Derivatives are all based on the prices of the other assets we discussed above: currencies, bonds, equities, and commodities. Investing in derivatives is an advanced and complicated way of making money on price changes in these other asset classes.

Typically, the price of a derivative is linked to the price of its underlying asset. As the underlying price moves up, a derivative that simulates ownership of the asset also moves up in price.

Are Derivatives Right For Me?

Some of these products make sense for individual investors. Many do not.

Typically, the risk involved in buying and selling derivatives is higher than the risk of buying the asset they're based on. Many professional asset managers have bought and sold derivatives without really understanding the risks they were running. Similarly, many banks have created products without really understanding the negative financial impact these products could have. Always use caution when dealing with derivatives.

In every case, derivatives and other products are not new asset classes in themselves. They all reflect the price movements of the underlying asset classes we discussed above.

If this has you feeling nervous, don't worry. Just sit tight for now! Once you become an expert in understanding and investing in all of the main asset classes, you'll be ready to delve into these other, more complicated products.

Guess what? We've finally reached the end of Module 4! I know it was a long one, but you did it.

Module 4 Top Tip: Primary vs. Secondary Market

Shares in a company can also be traded between investors. After an investor buys shares directly from the company on the primary market, he or she can then sell those shares to other investors on the secondary market.

The primary market is where securities are first issued. It's the capital market where businesses sell, or float, new stocks and bonds for the first time.

The secondary market, also known as the aftermarket, is the market on which securities are traded after the initial issuing of the security.

MODULE FIVE

People Power

Lesson One: Who's Who?

You learned a huge amount in Module 4. Congratulations! You're making awesome progress.

So far, we've covered why we should invest ourselves, the ins and outs of the entire economy, and about all of the main asset classes.

In this module, we're going to learn about the most important factor in financial markets: people.

Financial markets are all about people. Human decisions, emotions, and psychology play a big role in financial markets (as they do in any marketplace).

There are many groups of people who impact and participate in the markets. In each lesson, we'll go over:

1. Who is the market player?
2. What do they do in the market?
3. How do their actions affect the markets?

Ready to go? Feeling good? Then let's get started!

Lesson Two: Politicians

Most politics in a liberal democracy come down to three big issues:

1. What is the role of government?
2. How big should it be?
3. Who pays for it?

Politicians decide the role of the government in relation to the economy. Some governments let the market stay free and minimally regulated. Other governments decide to regulate markets more closely. Both will affect the economy in some way.

Let's take a look at what politicians do in the market and how political actions affect the market.

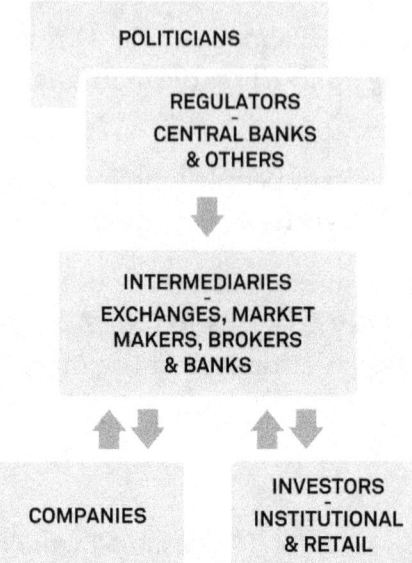

Government Spending

Every politician has a different idea of how much the government should spend and what to spend it on. As we learned in Module 3, the more a government spends, the larger the economy gets. Increased government spending can increase the revenue of businesses, growing these businesses and raising their value.

For example: if the government decides to spend more money on healthcare, healthcare stocks will do well. Other government spending can increase the wealth of households, allowing them to spend more in the economy and boosting market demand.

Price Controls

Some governments have laws that create minimum or maximum prices for goods in an economy.

Minimum wage laws are a great example. These laws set a minimum price for how much businesses pay workers in the labor market. The higher the minimum wage, the higher the cost for businesses, but the more money households in the economy make.

Other price controls, like price ceilings, set the maximum price a seller can charge for a good. Some cities like San Francisco have rent control laws, which limit rent to a maximum price in certain apartments. These controls can change the market price of goods as well as the incomes of businesses and households in the economy.

Trade

Politicians also determine our relations with foreign countries. This includes who we trade with and on what terms. As we learned in Module 3, good foreign trade relations are good for the economy and the financial markets. Bad foreign relations can decrease international trade and hurt the economy, especially if the economy is not diversified. Some global organizations, like the World Trade Organization, have been developed to help foster and oversee mutually beneficial trade agreements.

Taxes

Politicians don't just decide how much money the government spends and what it's spent on. They also set tax rates.

The government needs these taxes to fund itself and the programs described above. These can include:

1. Taxes on corporations: government taxation on businesses is a large source of revenue for government spending. Changes in the rates at which companies are taxed will have direct and significant impacts on these companies and their value. For example: if the government decides to raise taxes on technology companies, technology stocks will fall. Conversely, if the government decides to lower the tax rate on technology companies, tech stocks will rise.
2. Taxes on households: along with taxing businesses, governments also tax households to generate revenue.

Changing these tax rates also affects the economy and markets. For example: the government may apply a tax on purchases of soda; this will decrease sales of soda, but boost other companies in the drinks market.

3. Tariffs: tariffs are taxes on imports. These tariffs generate money for the government and can be used to regulate trade and alter the trade balance.

For example: if the US government imposes a tariff on car imports, they add an extra tax on all consumer purchases of cars made outside the US. This encourages US consumers to buy American cars instead of foreign cars, and improves the American trade balance. However, these tariffs will hurt the foreign companies exporting these goods as well as the US consumers who still want to buy foreign cars.

Lesson Three: Central Bankers

Central bankers are the people in charge of the national central bank. They control our national currency and our monetary policy.

The Fed

In the US, the central bank is called the Federal Reserve, and is considered the most powerful central bank in the world. The Federal Reserve, or Fed as it's commonly known, was set up in 1913. Its task is to maximize jobs in the economy and keep inflation under control. The Fed also supervises and regulates banks.

The Fed is managed by a Board of Governors appointed by the President. These seven governors together with twelve regional Fed chairmen make up the Federal Open Markets Committee or

FOMC.

The Fed's Role in the Markets

Remember, the Fed has two key aims: keep inflation under control and maintain a stable economy. To decide on the right actions to reach these goals, the FOMC meets approximately every six weeks.

At these meetings, the Fed decides which monetary policy tool it'll use to achieve its aims for the economy. Two tools the Fed has used most often in recent years are:

1. Interest rates: changing interest rates is the most common monetary policy tool. The Fed uses interest rates to make sure that the economy grows at a steady pace. This helps prevent both negative growth and recessions, but also rapid growth, which could lead to dangerously high inflation. To do this, the Fed looks at the current trajectory of the economy. If the economy is too strong and inflation is too high, it puts interest rates up, which slows down economic activity. If the economy is too slow or inflation is too low, it lowers interest rates, which speeds up economic activity. When the Fed raises interest rates, the equity markets normally fall, because it gets more expensive for companies to borrow and grow. When the Fed lowers interest rates, the markets normally rise, because it gets cheaper for companies to borrow and grow.
2. Open market operations: a newer monetary policy tool, open market operations came to the forefront during the 2008 financial crisis. During the crisis, the Fed bought a massive volume of securities, including bonds and toxic debt, from private banks. This helped banks get rid of assets that were hurting them and increased the amount of money these banks had. This money then gave people and businesses more access to

loans to help themselves recover from the recession, and also increased the level of inflation.

In times when the economy is too strong and inflation is too high, the Fed will sell bonds instead of buying them, decreasing the amount of money in the economy. This slows down lending by banks and lowers inflation.

The Fed's decisions, as shown above, directly influence whether the economy will grow faster or slower. As a result, the Fed has a great influence over the markets, and FOMC decisions are closely watched by all investors, whether they're large banks or individual investors.

Lesson Four: Regulators and SROs

Part of the Fed's job is to regulate banks. But there are lots of financial firms (like brokers) that aren't banks. So, who gets to regulate them?

Regulators and SROs

Instead of the Fed, the Securities Exchange Commission (SEC) or the Commodity Futures Trading Commission (CFTC) are the two regulatory agencies created and run by the US government to regulate firms that aren't banks.

These regulators also delegate some of their powers to regulatory agencies that are *not* governmental agencies, called Self-Regulating Organizations (SROs). The SRO responsible for the securities markets is called the Financial Industry Regulatory Authority (FINRA).

What Do Regulatory Agencies Do?

Regulators make sure financial markets are fair and orderly.

They also maintain strict control over what financial firms can and can't do. Responsibilities include:

- Enforcing rules around the issuance of new securities in the marketplace
- Regulating how the secondary markets operate
- Enforcing rules around how and when companies can report important information to the public

These regulations also ensure that smaller savers and investors are treated fairly by everyone else.

More recently, regulators have focused on the cryptocurrency markets and Initial Coin Offerings. In many countries, regulators have banned trading in cryptocurrencies and have taken legal action against ICOs. The reason? To control the pace of innovation and standards of conduct in the financial markets.

How Do Regulatory Actions Affect Markets?

Regulatory agencies have significant effects on how the markets operate. When firms don't act in line with the rules set out by these agencies, they put both themselves and the entire market at risk. When government regulators and SROs are successful, they can close down dishonest brokers to ensure the market remains healthy and free of financial crime.

When regulators aren't successful, markets can break down. For over 40 years, Bernie Madoff ran one of the most successful Ponzi schemes in history, stealing over $18 billion from investors before the SEC could finally arrest him. More recently, Einar Aas, an investor in Norway, "blew a hole" in the NASDAQ through risky trades that cost the exchange over $100 million.

Regulators are super necessary for the markets to run smoothly. For the rest of this module, we'll look at the people who make up these markets.

Lesson Five: Exchanges

Exchanges are the digital marketplaces where trading of securities occurs. They're one of the most important parts of the financial system!

What kind of securities are we talking about? There could be securities that already exist and are "listed" for trading on the exchange. Or they could be new securities, like an Initial Public Offering (IPO), where a company is being listed for the first time.

What Do Exchanges Do in the Market?

Stock exchanges process millions of transactions every day. In order to do this, they have sophisticated technology called matching engines that electronically match buyers and sellers of the same security.

All trades that go through exchanges are published. Every exchange is required to submit its trade data to a unified price feed.

In the US, this price feed is used to calculate the National Best Bid or Offer (NBBO). Regulation forces brokers to transact for clients at the best possible price. For example, if a broker is buying a share for his client, he must buy the share from the seller with the cheapest asking price. Similarly, if he's selling a share for his client, he must sell that share to the buyer with the highest bid.

Exchanges monitor all of the trading activity to ensure that there are no suspicious transactions taking place. They look for patterns that suggest insider trading (illegal trading by company directors and other insiders). They also enforce rules about company announcements and other reporting requirements. This is all to make sure that the markets remain fair and transparent for all investors.

Exchanges are open for defined hours of the day. For example: the NYSE is open from 9.30am to 4pm daily, although some limited trading takes place outside these hours. Every exchange in every country has different trading hours, so it's important to be aware of the hours.

How Do Exchanges Make Money?

Exchanges make money from the markets by charging users small transaction fees. To encourage people to add to the liquidity, they charge people who actively offer to buy or sell securities less than people who only accept existing offers.

Exchanges also make money by selling data to banks, brokers, and other participants. This data is a feed of all the transaction prices.

Lesson Six: Market Makers

Exchanges rely on traders to post the prices at which they're willing to buy or sell securities. These are called Bid and Asks:

- Bids (for buying)
- Asks or offers (for selling)

The more bids and offers there are, the greater the chance of an investor being able to buy or sell the securities they want at an agreeable price. The ability to buy or sell an asset on the market is called liquidity.

Depending on the size and popularity of the underlying company, liquidity will vary from one company to another. The most liquid securities tend to be the largest companies by valuation, because their shares are the most frequently traded (meaning there are constantly new bids and offers made for these stocks from investors).

There's a kind of trader called a market maker who specializes in posting bids and offers on the exchange. Once, they used to be physically present on the floor of the exchange. Now, most market makers operate electronically, using computers to post their prices.

The Market Maker's Role

Market makers want to trade simultaneously with different clients who want to buy and sell the same security. They make money by capturing the difference in price between the bid and the offer. To do this successfully, they need to have as much volume of trades as possible. If they can, they'll match buy and sell orders before they trade on the exchange.

How do they make money? Market makers pay some firms for their orders and make money from their clients. That is why these firms are able to offer "free" brokerage. Many of their trades never make it to the exchange. Instead, the market makers make a nice profit from the orders.

High Frequency Traders

Some market makers can also be referred to as High Frequency Traders. They use sophisticated models to calculate tiny differences in mean reversion or momentum, and update their bids and offers in nanoseconds. This allows them to maximize their profit. They also compete to build super-fast connectivity to the exchanges.

If it sounds exciting, that's because it is! You could say market making has become the financial market equivalent of a technology arms race.

Lesson Seven: Brokers

Brokers are the people who receive client orders and send them to the marketplace. They earn commissions from clients for executing their orders. Unlike market makers, brokers don't take risk on their client orders.

Types of Brokers

Brokers come in all flavors. Most are called introducing brokers. Introducing brokers don't hold or control client cash or securities. Instead, they introduce their clients to carrying brokers, who are responsible for looking after client funds, processing trades, and keeping client securities safe.

Another major type of broker is an executing broker. They're a member of the exchange and are responsible for executing any trades sent to them by an introducing or carrying broker.

How Brokers Execute Trades

The execution of these deals could take place on exchanges, or it could be via a market maker off the exchange. In every case, regulators require that the trades are executed in accordance with the NBBO. This protects individual investors, since it ensures all deals completed by brokers will have been for the best available price.

Broker firms (especially large ones owned by banks) can also bring new issues or IPOs to the market. Typically, an investment banker advises a company on the right strategy to issue shares. An Equity Capital Markets expert advises on the price and timing of the offering. Salespeople help sell the IPO. Research analysts publish research on the new security.

Successful IPOs trade at a higher price to their new issue price as other investors look to buy in to the new company's stock. A healthy IPO market is a sign that the market is strong.

How Their Actions Affect the Market

Brokers compete with other brokers for commissions. One way they do this is to offer their clients price data, market analysis, or research. Research is carefully regulated, because broker research recommendations can have a big impact on the price of a security.

Lesson Eight: Companies

The main purpose of the financial markets (and of the banking system in general) is to facilitate the flow of money from people who want to invest to those who need capital to grow. Financial markets are like the beating heart of a capitalist economy. Efficient capital markets lead to growth, employment, and prosperity.

The main recipients of that capital are companies. Companies employ people, buy equipment, and offer goods and services in the economy. They're important drivers of economic activity.

When we think about the stock market now, we typically think about companies that have listed their shares for the public to buy. In total, as of 2020, the value of all companies listed on exchanges around the world exceeds $85 trillion. The sum of all debt in the world, including government debt is about $250 trillion!

The Role of Companies in the Market

Companies regularly perform corporate actions. Corporate actions impact the shares in the market. They include:

1. Share issuance
2. Stock-splits
3. Reverse-splits

4. Mergers and acquisitions
5. Share buyback
6. Paying a dividend

Share Issuance

Companies use the stock market to issue new shares. This could be in the form of an IPO. If they want to raise more capital after the IPO, they can also issue more shares.

Selling equity to raise capital is called a primary sale. Selling even more equity on the primary market when a company is already publicly listed is called a follow-on offering.

Don't confuse this with the secondary market, though: follow-on offerings are equity sales directly from the company on the primary market, whereas trade of shares between investors is done in the secondary market.

Mergers and Acquisitions

When one company buys another listed company, the stock of the company being acquired will be delisted from the exchange, meaning it's taken off of the stock exchange. When companies merge, one of the two companies will also be delisted. The remaining company might also be re-named or re-branded.

Share Buyback

Sometimes, companies buy back their shares from the marketplace. In 2018, US companies bought back over $1.1 trillion of their shares! They did this to boost their returns; a company that makes $100 on $1000 of outstanding stock will generate a return of 10% on its market value. If it buys back 20% of its shares, leaving only $800 in outstanding stock, it can boost its returns from 10% to 12.5% of market value, since it'll make $100 on only $800 of outstanding stock.

Buybacks can also help to drive up the price of a company's stock, as the number of shares in the market will decrease, making the remaining shares more in demand.

Companies are important players in the stock market. It's good to know what insiders are doing with their shares and to understand the intentions of the company that issues or buys back its stock.

Lesson Nine: Institutional Investors

Institutional investors are the businesses and people who manage large sums of money on behalf of many different types of clients.

Institutional Investor Types

Institutional investors come in all shapes and sizes. Let's take a look at a few of them.

Sovereign Wealth Funds (SWFs) manage money on behalf of governments. For example: Norway has one of the biggest SWFs managing the surplus money generated from oil sales for its population. The assets of SWFs can be trillions of dollars.

Asset managers manage investment portfolios on behalf of companies or other institutional investors.

For example: an asset manager might manage part of a company's pension plan. Asset managers tend to tailor each portfolio to the needs of their individual clients.

Mutual funds provide a single portfolio that investors can buy or sell. Each mutual fund provides exposure to a set of opportunities.

For example: one mutual fund might invest in large technology companies, another in healthcare stocks, while a third might invest in emerging markets. Individual investors can buy or sell mutual funds on a daily basis, typically at the closing price of the fund.

Pension funds manage money that has been set aside to provide pensions for workers when they retire or stop working. A pension is income that a retired person continues to receive usually until they die.

In a defined benefit fund, the pensioners receive a defined pension after they stop working, regardless of the performance of the fund. In a defined contribution scheme, the pension payable to all beneficiaries is subject to the overall performance of that fund.

Insurance companies collect insurance premiums in return for paying out benefits in the event of certain risks occurring, like theft, fire, health-related, death, etc. Although we pay premiums to these insurance companies to protect us, the amount they pay out when these events occur is often more than the fees we pay them.

In order to earn a profit, insurance companies invest the premiums policyholders pay in the markets. This lets them generate a return to pay out to their policyholders if the risks do occur. Life insurance companies in particular tend to be long-term investors.

Exchange Traded Funds are passively managed listed funds that provide investors with exposure to a particular set of underlying stocks that remains mostly constant over time.

For example: SPDR invests in all 500 companies listed in the S&P 500 index. This makes it more convenient for an individual investor to buy a single ETF rather than one share of each of the 500 companies. Other ETFs give exposure to other sectors, regions, or strategies. Robo-advisors typically invest only in ETFs.

Hedge funds are supposedly highly skilled asset managers who charge higher fees for their services. While most asset managers charge 1% of the assets being managed, hedge fund managers usually charge 2% of the funds being managed annually, plus 20% of the returns they generate. These higher fees are normally due to the high returns that hedge funds generate, as they often operate using high-risk, high-reward trades and investments.

Hedge funds cater towards high-net-worth individuals who must buy into the fund with a large minimum investment. These investments must also typically stay in the hedge fund for a longer period of time, and the process of taking one's money out of the fund is more difficult than with other asset managers or with a mutual fund.

Institutional Investors in the Market

All asset managers have an investment mandate and an investment style. Their mandate will specify what they can invest in. For example, they could invest in US equities or international equities. Or they could be focused on emerging markets or small companies.

Sometimes, they'll be benchmarked against an index like the S&P 500 and expected to perform better than that index. To do this, their mandate will give them some flexibility to depart from the index.

Hedge funds have the most flexible mandates. They can typically buy or sell most assets. This gives the most opportunity to generate a higher return.

Most institutional investors tend to favor certain investment styles. For example, they could have a mandate to invest in auto companies. Their style might be to pick companies that are trading cheaply relative to their peers or those with strong momentum.

There are many different mandates and styles in the financial markets. That means that people will be buying and selling for very different reasons. All of these different activities result in a continual push and pull in financial asset prices as institutional investors choose to buy or sell large quantities of securities in high-volume transactions.

Lesson Ten: Retail Investors

The last category of people in the markets is the most important - all of us! We're known as retail investors.

Not all retail investors are created equal. Those with certain levels of income or wealth are called accredited investors. They're allowed to buy fewer liquid securities that other retail investors aren't allowed to buy.

Regulation

The amount that a retail investor can borrow against his or her portfolio is also regulated. Regulation T prevents margin lending of more than 50%.

Regulations designed to protect retail investors can sometimes prevent them from getting access to information and opportunities that other investors expect to have.

How Retail Investors Affect the Markets

We expect retail investors to become an increasingly powerful part of the markets.

For a long time, the financial industry created a myth that financial markets are so complicated that they require professional expertise to navigate. This self-justifying argument was the rationale for the industry to charge high fees to manage other people's money.

Study after study has shown that institutional investors are not that great at managing money. As a community, they underperform the markets and their benchmarks over time. Some might get lucky in the short term, but over time, you would be better served managing your money yourself.

Overall, we think that retail investors will increasingly take charge of their own investments rather than pay someone else high fees to underperform the market.

Retail Investors and The Future

Although individual investors may not have the same amount of capital to invest in the markets as institutional investors do, we still make up a significant percentage of trading activity, which is increasing every day as young people invest more.

However, many retail investors are less successful than they can be - often, because they do not educate themselves on *how* to invest. But hey, you're here! That means you're ahead of the pack already.

Lesson Eleven: A Word on Fintech Disruptors

Fintech isn't about finance. It's not even about technology.

It's about people.

In the financial markets, Fintech is the manifestation of the information revolution that's already taking place in other sectors of the economy, like media, travel, entertainment, and transport.

The information revolution has taken information and power out of the hands of the old institutions (nation states, governments, political parties, banks, media companies, universities) and put it into the hands of individuals. Think about how Instagram turned us all into photographers, or how Airbnb our homes into potential hotels, or how Uber turned every car into a potential taxi. You've got the power.

How Fintech Firms Affect Us

Fintech firms empower individuals to take charge of their own financial destinies by giving them access to the information and opportunities that other institutional investors historically had.

Banks, brokers, and asset managers (people who get between you and your money) are getting squeezed by Fintech disruptors. Fintech firms have given us closer access to our bank accounts, brokerage accounts, and financial education than ever before. Thanks to advances in Fintech, we're now in the driver's seat of our own financial futures.

Module 5 Top Tip: Exchange Traded Funds

Institutional investors are the businesses and people who manage large sums of money on behalf of many different types of clients. One kind of institutional investor is an Exchange Traded Fund. Unlike mutual funds, which are traded only once a day after the market closes, Exchange Traded Funds or ETFs are a basket of securities that trade on an exchange throughout the day, just like a stock.

MODULE SIX

Worldly Wisdom

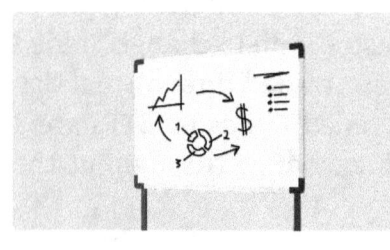

Lesson One: Introduction

Congrats, you've made it this far! I know it's a lot of info, but you're crushing it.

In this module, we're finally going to start putting together everything we've learned so we can understand the financial markets in a single coherent framework.

Let's recap:

- In Module 4, we looked at the factors that cause the

prices of assets in each asset class to go up and down.
- In Module 5, we looked at the different players in a market and what effects they have on the markets.

Now, we'll combine everything we've learned to understand how all the players in a market can change the prices of different assets, and how the financial markets work as a whole.

Ready? Of course you are. Let's go!

Lesson Two: Politics

We've already learned that financial markets are all about people. And who are the people with the most power?

Politicians

We give politicians the authority to manage the country on our behalf. Their decisions impact what the government spends money on, how much it spends, and who has to pay for it.

That's a pretty big deal.

As such, government spending has a huge impact on the economy. It also affects different parts of the economy, like the healthcare system, education, and defense industries. Governments also employ a lot of people, both directly and indirectly, adding to their economic impact.

In total, in the US, the government accounts for over 40% of all economic activity. In the UK, the government accounts for almost 50% of all economic activity while in France, it accounts for over 50%.

As a result of all this spending, all political actions, big or small, have a direct impact on the economy in some way.

Government Spending

As you already know, government spending affects our economy, and changing the level of government spending will change the rate of economic growth. If government spending increases, the economy will grow. Similarly, if government spending in a certain sector increases, that sector of the economy will grow.

For example: if the government reduces military spending and raises agricultural spending, the military sector of the economy will shrink and share prices for defense companies will fall. Meanwhile, the agricultural sector and share prices of agriculture firms will rise.

Government Taxation

Government taxation also affects our economy. If taxes are raised, the government will have more money to spend, but this will be taken from the budgets of either companies or households. This causes the economy to slow down overall, as household and business spending will both decrease.

If more taxes are taken from companies, share prices of these companies will fall due to lower profits. If more taxes are taken from households, they'll have less to spend, and share prices in companies producing consumer goods will fall. However, share prices in companies that sell to the government will rise, as the government will have more tax revenue to spend.

The opposite will happen if the government cuts taxes: the economy will grow as businesses throughout the market see their share prices increase, but businesses that sell to the government will see their sales fall, because the government has less tax revenue to spend.

Fiscal Policy

Whenever we're analyzing any market, one of the first questions we should ask is whether the government is supporting economic growth by spending money or slowing it down by increasing taxes. This balance between spending and taxation is called fiscal policy. Understanding fiscal policy is an important first step in understanding how the financial markets are likely to behave.

Lesson Three: What is Fiscal Policy?

After the Great Depression of 1929, British economist John Maynard Keynes developed a theory that later became known as Keynesian economics. This theory states that when households and companies lack the courage to invest, governments should step in to help support the economy by filling in the holes.

For example: when businesses fired workers to cut costs in the Great Depression (causing the unemployment rate to skyrocket to nearly 25%), Keynes' theory prompted the government to fill this gap in the economy by employing tens of thousands of unemployed workers to complete construction projects for the government in federal work programs. Governments that spend money when other people are afraid to do so are said to be acting counter-cyclically.

However, there are also times when government spending competes for resources within an already-strong economy. If the economy is already growing and unemployment is low, then increased demand is more likely to push up prices, rather than boost real economic activity.

To see why, let's go back to your friend Emma's lemonade business. Imagine the economy is booming and Emma's producing all of the lemonade she can. A government officer comes by and wants to buy six crates of Emma's lemonade. In response, Emma will likely increase the price of her lemonade.

Why?

Emma can't increase her production to sell more lemonade at the current price because she's already producing the maximum that she can. So, instead of encouraging Emma to create more output, the increased demand from the government just increases prices for the lemonade she currently sells.

As this example shows, increasing government spending during a period of strong economic growth doesn't actually help the economy. Instead, it pushes prices up and causes higher levels of inflation, which can hurt consumers.

When governments spend more money in an economy that's already strong, it's called pro-cyclical fiscal policy. Chances are, pro-cyclical fiscal policy will push up prices more than it will stimulate real economic activity.

However, increases in spending don't have to be directly from the government. The other way for governments to influence economic activity is to lower taxes on companies and households. Lower taxes mean more money left in peoples' pockets to spend, which boosts the economy in much the same way that government spending does. So, lower taxes is a way for the government to help the economy indirectly.

In aggressive forms of fiscal policy, a government can combine both government spending increases and tax cuts to rapidly speed economic growth. Though this type of fiscal policy can be successful in helping an economy recover from a deep hole (like the 2008 financial crisis), this can also cause an economy to grow too fast. In this case, if the economy "overheats" due to too much pro-cyclical fiscal policy, the government can actually drive a strong economy into a recession as a result of high inflation.

Fiscal policy is only one side of the government's handle on the economy. In the next lesson, we'll look again at monetary policy and the central bank, and how it affects the economy and markets.

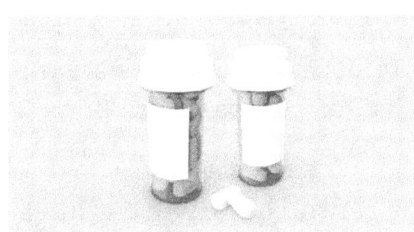

Lesson Four: What is Monetary Policy?

In Module 5, we learned that the most powerful people in the economy after politicians are central bankers. Politicians control fiscal policy. But central bankers control the level of interest rates in the economy. This is called monetary policy.

In many countries, central bankers are appointed by politicians. They're then free to manage monetary policy independently of the government. In the US, the President appoints the Fed governors, who then decide what the level of interest rates should be.

If they had the choice, most politicians would prefer interest rates to be as low as possible to encourage borrowing, spending, investing, and economic growth. This would make them more likely to get re-elected.

Because of this, central banks are independent so they can set the appropriate level of interest rates for an economy. This means politicians can't influence central bank decisions. The central bank's job is to maintain levels of inflation and economic growth that are stable and healthy. It's not their job to get politicians re-elected.

The Fed's Job

In the US, the Fed's job is to manage both economic growth and inflation. As such, when setting monetary policy, the Fed must consider both the level of economic activity and the level of inflation. They try to look as far forward as possible to anticipate future events that will cause changes in either economic growth or inflation. This allows them to prepare policies that can counter these events.

If the central bank thinks the economy is overheating, it'll raise interest rates. This encourages saving and discourages lending and investment, causing the economy to slow down. Often, the stock market will fall when interest rate increases are announced, because it's more expensive for companies to borrow money to expand their business.

If the economy is slowing down, the central bank will cut interest rates. This encourages lending and investment, and discourages saving, causing the economy to speed up. This also causes share prices to rise since it makes company borrowing cheaper, allowing for more investment and expansion of businesses.

Consider what central banks around the world did in response to the 2008 financial crisis. Interest rates were held extremely low for many years after the crisis, as central banks tried to increase spending and grow the economy in the wake of a terrible recession.

Federal Funds Rate

When we talk about interest rates, what we're really talking about is the rate at which the central bank lends money to other commercial banks. The Fed is like the bankers' banker. Other banks can deposit money with the Fed, or the Fed can allow banks to lend excess deposits to each other using the Federal funds rate.

Banks who want to borrow money from the Fed place government bonds as collateral with the Fed and borrow money at the Federal reserve rate. Commercial banks can also lend money to each other at the Fed funds rate. These loans are often done on an overnight basis. In practice, the Fed and other central banks do not influence all interest rates, but only these short-term rates.

In the next lesson, we'll look at long-term interest rates and how they affect the market.

Lesson Five: Long-term Interest Rates

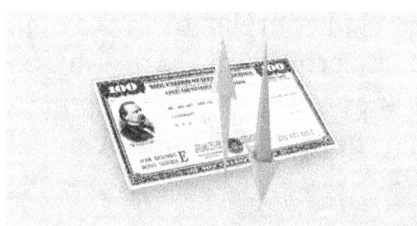

If someone asked you to lend them money for one day, you might charge them 2%. If they asked you to lend them money for ten years, you'd probably want to charge them a higher rate of interest. That's because you might have more uses for your money over ten years than overnight. Plus, there's always the chance that they might be less likely to pay you back in ten years than tomorrow.

As you can see, the rates at which banks lend or borrow vary depending on how long the loan is for. Short-term loans are normally at lower interest rates. Long-term loans have higher interest rates.

Yield Curve

The different levels of interest rates are referred to as a yield curve. A yield curve plots interest rates on the y axis and time on the x axis. Because interest rates normally get higher as the term of the loan gets longer, we expect to see the yield curve rising from left to right on the chart.

One of the main ways banks make money is by borrowing on a short-term basis and lending money out on a longer-term basis. They're able to capture the difference between short-term and long-term interest rates by doing this, making a profit on this spread.

When short-term interest rates are low relative to long-term interest rates, banks will buy longer-term bonds. This is because the bank can make more money from investing in bonds with high interest rates than lending to others at lower interest rates. As more banks buy bonds and increase the market demand for bonds, bond prices will increase and bond yields will fall.

The converse is true when short-term interest rates are high relative to long-term interest rates. Banks prefer to make high returns by earning interest on short-term loans, and will buy fewer bonds. This decreases the market demand for bonds, lowering bond prices and increasing the yield of bonds overall.

Lesson Six: Foreign Exchange Rates

In Module 4, we learned that foreign exchange rates are the price between two national currencies. Increased demand for the base currency relative to the quoted currency makes the foreign exchange rate go up.

Long-Term Interest Rates

One of the main drivers of demand for a currency is the level of long-term interest rates in that country.

For example: if you know that you can earn more money by investing in long-term American bonds denominated in US dollars than in long-term Japanese bonds denominated in Japanese yen, you would want to buy US dollars and sell Japanese yen. Everything else being equal, the USDJPY exchange rate is likely to go up when long-term US interest rates go up, or long-term Japanese interest rates go down.

Conversely, a fall in US long-term interest rates or a rise in long-term Japanese interest rates will cause the USDJPY exchange rate to fall, and the USD to become less valuable relative to the JPY.

So, long-term interest rates affect foreign exchange rates. Higher long-term interest rates in one country will tend to boost that country's exchange rate relative to another country's.

When the Fed puts up interest rates, we normally expect bond yields to rise. Higher bond yields attract foreign investors who buy the US dollar and sell their local currency, causing the exchange rate to shift and the US dollar to become more expensive relative to the local currency.

Foreign Exchange Rates and the Global Trade Balance

This change in the foreign exchange rate also changes the global trade balance: how much each country imports and exports. If long-term interest rates in the US go up, demand for long-term American bonds rise and the price of the US dollar will increase.

For example: if a German wants to buy American goods, she must first buy US dollars. If the price of the US dollar increases relative to the euro, this will make American goods more expensive for the German, and she'll buy fewer of them. However, Americans will be able to buy *more* German goods, since the euro will have become cheaper relative to the US dollar.

As a result, as long-term interest rates increase in a country, that country will see its exports fall and imports rise, creating a more negative trade balance. The opposite is true when long-term interest rates fall: the value of the US dollar falls relative to other countries, creating a more positive trade balance as exports rise and imports fall.

This change in net exports affects the global economy directly. If American net exports decrease, the US imports more and exports less, leading to an increase in the revenues of foreign companies and a decrease in the revenues of American companies.

The opposite is true if American exports increase and imports decrease: American companies' revenues will increase and foreign companies' revenues will decrease.

This is largely why Chinese companies have been so successful in the 21st century: a strong US dollar, coupled with a weak Chinese yuan, has led to a trade balance between the US and China where the US mostly imports and China mostly exports. This has driven not only the growth of China's economy, but also rapid rises in the market capitalizations and stock prices of many of China's biggest companies.

Lesson Seven: Commodities

We've just learned how changes in fiscal policy can change monetary policy. We've also seen how changes in monetary policy and interest rates can cause changes in the economy as well as the markets for currency and bonds.

In the next three lessons, we'll see how these changes affect the markets for the three remaining asset classes: commodities, equities, and cryptocurrencies.

Commodities

In Module 4, we learned that many commodities are priced in US dollars. Many commodity producers are located in emerging markets all around the world. Commodity producers convert the US dollars they earn into local currency to pay workers locally.

As the US dollar rises in value against other currencies, each dollar that commodity producers earn converts into more local currency. So, commodity producers get richer. Commodity producers are generally willing to sell more commodities because they're earning more money locally.

By contrast, commodity consumers outside the US get poorer as the US dollar rises; they need to spend more local currency to buy the same amount of US dollars that they need to buy the commodities. As a result, they try to buy fewer commodities when the US dollar goes up.

When the US dollar becomes more expensive relative to other currencies, it's getting stronger. When the US dollar becomes cheaper, it's getting weaker.

A stronger US dollar pushes up the supply and pushes down the demand for commodities, causing commodity prices to fall.

A weaker US dollar decreases supply and increases demand for commodities, causing commodity prices to rise.

We can use this intuition to look at changes in the oil price. A weak US dollar in the summer of 2011 saw surging gas prices in the US, with drivers having to pay over $4/gallon to fill their car's gas tank. Yet, in the summer of 2019, the US dollar was very strong compared with most world currencies, leading to gas prices falling under $2/gallon in some places in the US! Currency prices alone can drive large changes in the commodities market.

Lesson Eight: Equities

The share prices of commodity producers and consumers can also be affected by the movements in US dollars. Higher local currency earnings mean higher profits in local currency terms.

The UK stock market has a lot of international commodity companies listed on the London Stock Exchange. These include large oil companies like BP and Shell, as well as large metal and mining companies like Anglo American and BHP Billiton.

When the US dollar rises or commodity prices rise, the value of these companies also rises. This pushes up the value of the UK stock market overall. Equity markets in commodity-producing countries rise. They fall in commodity-consuming countries.

Emerging market countries tend to do better when the US dollar is falling since many emerging market countries are commodity producers. Emerging countries also tend to borrow money in US dollars, so their debts become cheaper when the US dollar falls.

Other Factors

Different equity sectors are affected by other factors such as interest rates. Companies with a lot of debt, like real estate companies, do better when interest rates fall. Banks, which are quick to charge borrowers more when interest rates rise and slow to pass on higher deposit rates, do better when interest rates rise.

Different sectors are also impacted by the economic cycle. As the economy is recovering early in the economic cycle, consumer discretionary, real estate, and materials stocks do well. As interest rates start to rise later in the cycle, financial, technology, and communication stocks tend to do better. As the economy slows down and interest rates fall, consumer staples, health care, and utility stocks perform better than other sectors.

All of these rules are general guidelines; they may differ slightly from economic cycle to economic cycle. Still, they're a good place to start when doing your research.

Lesson Nine: Cryptocurrencies

Cryptocurrencies are a relatively new asset class. As we saw in Module 4, they're not impacted by the same factors that affect other asset classes (interest rates, the yield curve, exchange rates). In fact, one of the great benefits of cryptocurrencies is that they're uncorrelated to other asset classes. This means that a portfolio that has cryptocurrencies is more diversified than one that does not have cryptocurrencies.

When faith in the old fiat system falls and equity markets have fallen, cryptocurrencies rise. When the equity markets rise, cryptocurrencies fall. This can help stock owners hedge their portfolios against market downturns: even if the stock market falls, the cryptocurrencies they hold will gain in value.

Following Cryptocurrencies

The best way to follow the cryptocurrency market is to use an index like the Invstr Crypto Index - it makes it a lot easier to understand what's happening in the crypto world.

Tying It All Together

We've seen how the markets interconnect, from government to mainstream financial markets to cryptocurrencies. Below, we can see a diagram that shows how it all links together. With this in mind, the next module will look at how we can use our knowledge of this framework to begin analyzing and understanding the markets.

Wow, you just completed Module 6! We're super impressed with your progress. Keep crushing it.

Module 6 Top Tip: Monetary Policy

In Module 5, we learned that the most powerful people in the economy after politicians are central bankers. Politicians control fiscal policy, which is the means by which a government adjusts its spending levels and tax rates to guide and stabilize a country's economy.

Central bankers control the level of interest rates in the economy. This is called monetary policy. It's a macroeconomic policy meant to keep the economy strong and stable. The main monetary policy tools of a central bank are changing the base rate and the money supply.

MODULE SEVEN

Financial Fitness

Lesson One: Getting Financially Fit

You're in the home stretch! You've completed all the theory. You've also learned about a simple business; the whole economy; what makes financial markets go up and down; all the people who influence the financial markets; and how everything in the world is connected to everything else. Phew!

From this point on, it's all about practice. You'll learn what you need to do to get financially fit; how to create an investment process; how to open a brokerage account; and finally, some top tips about how to be a great investor in the real world.

Remember, learning to invest is like learning to play a sport or a musical instrument. To get good at investing, we have to do three things: get fit, practice, and perform.

Getting Financially Fit

In this module, we're going to focus on getting financially fit and practicing. (We'll tackle performing and investing at the top level in Module 8.) To get financially fit, we need to do three things:

1. Follow what's going on in the world
2. Watch how financial markets react to different news or events
3. Understand what other people are thinking

In the next few lessons, I'll take you through how to do each. This is a good time to download the Invstr app if you haven't already, as I'll also be showing you how Invstr helps you practice the above. Just head to your app store and search for "Invstr."

Ready? Let's go!

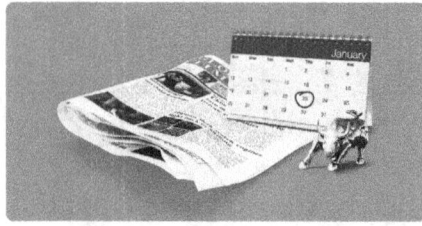

Lesson Two: Read the News & Check the Calendar

Everything that happens in the world affects the financial markets in some way. Even events that aren't clearly related to the economy have an effect on markets: the Olympics, for example, affects the economy of the host country and its national currency. These things can cause a chain reaction in financial markets; some may be small, but others can be so big they make worldwide news.

The more we understand what's going on in the world, the better we get at anticipating what could happen next. The best way to do that? Keep up with the news!

But just reading and reacting to the news isn't enough. Markets also try to anticipate what will happen next. That's why the markets sometimes react to news in ways we might not expect. In fact, we sometimes see the opposite reaction to what we expected!

How does this work? Sometimes, markets correctly anticipate news. When this happens, people want to profit from their predictions.

For example: a company might release great earnings. But instead of going up in value, the stock price falls! That's because the price had already risen in anticipation of those great earnings. When the news comes out, stockholders sell their holdings.

This is sometimes referred to as *buying the rumor and selling the fact.* These types of trades cause the market to react in the opposite way we would expect.

Reading the News on Invstr

At Invstr, we know it can be difficult and hectic trying to sift through the news to find what's important to investing. There are about 20,000 news articles alone on Invstr every single day!

To make it easier for you to get the information you need, we filter each news article to every instrument in the app, which you can read in the Instrument Hub Feed. This helps you stay updated on the instruments you care about, instead of sifting through news about every instrument.

You'll also find news stories in your Feed. Every hour, we post the stories we think are most relevant for you. This is based on your actions in the app and which instruments you have in your watchlist. Basically, the more you do on Invstr, the better we get at finding news stories that interest you! (You can also find news stories by using the Search feature in the Feed.)

One way to get ahead of the 'buying the rumor and selling the fact' trend is to check the Calendar (found in the Instrument Feed) for each instrument. The Calendar includes important dates like annual general meetings, company earnings results, dividend dates, etc. Checking the Calendar and being aware of upcoming news and events can help you stay ahead of the game.

Lesson Three: Watch How Prices Change

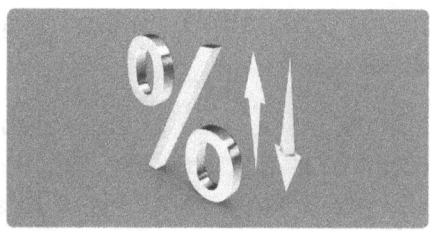

In addition to following the news, the next most important thing is to follow the price changes in the market. Ask yourself:

- Is the price going up or down?
- Did the price react the way I expected, given the news?
- If there was no news and the market still moved up or down, what caused it?

You may have heard the phrase *"the market is always right."*

Here's what that actually means: financial markets don't always react the way we expect them to. But the price is always the price at which a willing buyer and willing seller are prepared to trade. As a result, *there's always a reason for changes in market price*. Even if it's not clear why the price has risen or fallen, there must be a reason why the prices at which buyers or sellers were willing to make a trade has changed.

Learning from Price Changes

Understanding how prices change in relation to the news tells us a lot about what people were expecting. Remember: financial markets are all about people! The rules of thumb we learned in Module 4 and 6 are just guidelines. The market will do what it wants to do, no matter what the guidelines state.

For example: the US dollar becoming stronger usually means that commodity prices fall. But in 1998, commodity prices actually rose as the US dollar became stronger.

We can't always just rely on the rules we learn. Because of this, it's important to consider all factors when making an investment—especially those that might yield an unexpected result.

There's a lot we can learn by watching the price action. In fact, some people only follow the price action, because they say that this is all that matters. These people are called technical analysts. They think that market fundamentals, like the profitability of a company or the credit rating of a bond, are irrelevant.

At Invstr, we think a balanced approach is best. You can learn a lot more about the market if you know what should have happened and compare it to what actually happened.

If the news was good and the price went up, you can assume that the market is behaving normally. If the news was good and the market went down, maybe too many people already bought that instrument. If there was no news and the price went up, maybe people are starting to anticipate something. Or maybe there is someone who knows more than everyone else.

There's a reason behind every price movement. The key is discovering what that reason is and applying that knowledge to future investments.

Following Price Changes on Invstr

On Invstr, the price data is constantly updating or streaming to your phone. This means you don't need to constantly refresh! When an instrument moves more than normal, we automatically send out notifications to let you know that something unusual or important is happening. Make sure you have notifications turned on. Don't be the last to find out - it might be too late by then!

Again, markets are about people, and psychology is just as important as economics. Watching the markets regularly helps us learn a huge amount about the psychology of the markets.

Lesson Four: Use Charts to Put It in Context

Financial markets, like the economy, can go through cycles that last for years. Because of this, getting the hang of market conditions can take a long time. It can take years to experience all the different cycles and behaviors of the market!

Fortunately, there's a way to jump start the long process of gaining experience: we can look at price charts. Charts show prices over a period of time. That means that instead of looking just at the price right now, we can look back in time and see where the price has been.

What Charts Teach Us

By understanding where the price has been, we may be better prepared to think about where it could go next. Is the price trending (i.e. steadily moving up or down over time)? Or is the price range-bound (i.e. not really going anywhere)?

If the price is trending, what could be making that happen? If the price is range bound, what could make it start to move either up or down? If two instruments normally track each other and one is suddenly moving on its own, what has happened? Will it come back or will it keep on going its own way? We can begin to develop answers to these questions by analyzing the trends of charts.

Checking the Charts on Invstr

On Invstr, you can look back five years for any given instrument in the Instrument Hub. It's best to start with the longest time frame first and then move towards the shortest. Unfortunately, charts won't tell us what will happen next.

You can also compare two or more instruments over time. The Comparison Chart feature on Invstr lets you compare up to 5 instruments at any one time and look at their relative performance to each other.

Invstr also has a technical charting package. Technical analysis is a way of looking at price data to try to find clues about future price direction. Technical analysis uses statistical studies which fall into two main categories: trend following and mean reversion.

Trend following studies (like moving averages) try to determine if a trend is in place. Mean reversion studies (like Relative Strength Indicator) try to predict oversold or overbought market conditions.

Ultimately, prices matter and charts can help us put the current price into its historical context. We might not be fortune tellers, but understanding what has happened in the past is a great place to start.

Lesson Five: Check the Community Sentiment

Markets are about people: human psychology matters! If we could understand what everyone in the world was thinking, we'd be better prepared for what might happen next. Unfortunately, none of us can read minds (yet). Until then, we have a pretty good solution for solving the mystery of the markets...

Checking the Community Sentiment on Invstr

In the Instrument Hub, you'll find the overall community sentiment for each instrument. This means you can see whether more people are buying or selling. You can also see how many followers each instrument has, the number of games played, and the accuracy of the community when they buy or sell.

Another tip is to follow what the expert investors are doing. A good way to do this is to check the Invstr Fantasy League Leaderboard, where you'll see the top 100 Invstrs for the month listed. Their profiles will show historical performance, their investments, posts, and trades.

Following these top investors allows you to see all of their trades and posts in your own Feed, so you can easily see the trades and investments being made by the top investors out there. This is a great way to see what other people are thinking and doing—especially the successful ones—and how you might replicate and adapt their money moves.

Invstr also gives you the chance to invest and play with friends through our Private Leagues feature. Each Private League has a leaderboard that lets you see exactly how everyone is doing. You can also communicate with your league members via the group chat. Sometimes, more heads are better than one!

Knowing the community sentiment for each instrument adds to your understanding of what other people in the market are doing, and allows you to better predict future market changes and trends. It's not mind reading, but it's as close as you can get.

Lesson Six: Practice, Practice, Practice!

Researching and following other people is great, but there's nothing like doing things for yourself.

Practicing on Invstr

We totally get why you might be uneasy about investing in the stock market, especially if you're a beginner. That's why we created Fantasy Finance®! You can practice your investing skills in a real-world environment without risking any real money. Plus, no matter how badly you do in any one month, the game starts over again at the beginning of the next month!

We've also added some extra features to help you learn from your mistakes, like Safety Net and Undo a Trade. Safety Net lets you start each month with at least $1,000,000. Undo allows you to "undo" a really bad trade. These features let you use stock market simulations to practice and experiment, risk-free.

Finally, play with other people you know and learn from them. Follow people you don't already know and learn from them. Before you know it, you'll be ready for the big leagues.

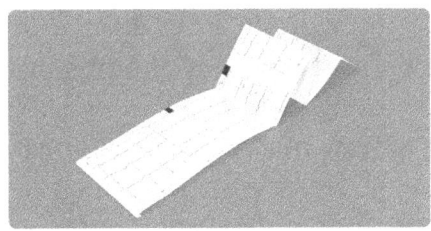

Lesson Seven: Build Your Track Record

Maybe you played a lot of sports or musical instruments when you were younger. There was always one you were better at over the others, right? Investing is similar. There are lots of different things to invest in, but you might be better at some over others because you have a natural affinity for certain sectors or commodities.

We become better investors when we play to our strengths. Track Record on Invstr helps us to understand some key things about our investing skills.

What Track Record Tells Us

The first thing Track Record can tell you is what kind of investor you are. We can look at this in two different ways: the things you like to invest in and what style of investing you have. Understanding these things is important to improving your performance.

The combination of things you like to invest in is called your investment mandate. On Track Record, your mandate is based on three things:

1. The sectors you invest in
2. The geography you invest in
3. The size (or market capitalization) of the companies you invest in

For example: if you like to invest in the FAANGs (Facebook, Apple, Amazon, Netflix and Google), your mandate is predominantly US, large capitalization, technology stocks.

Your *investing style* is determined by the characteristics of the companies you choose to invest in:

- Growth stocks: their sales or their revenues are growing fast (like Tesla)
- Momentum stocks: their share price is moving up steadily (like Netflix)
- Value stocks: they look cheap relative to their peer group (like Apple)
- Income stocks: they pay a nice dividend every quarter or every six months (like Ford)

Track Record also helps you learn how well you're doing. The most important gauge of performance is your return: the percentage performance you generate on your capital each month and over time.

Being a successful investor isn't just about generating the highest returns. It's also about generating returns consistently over time. Would you let someone manage your money if they made 10% one month but lost 9% next month? Or would you rather give your money to someone who made 4% returns consistently over time?

We measure consistency by looking at how predictable or volatile our returns are. When dividing our percentage returns by the volatility of those returns, we calculate a measure of consistency called a Sharpe ratio. Track Record tells you how well you're doing and measures your Sharpe ratio, and compares both of these measures against the community average.

Track Record also tells you two more valuable pieces of information about your investing performance: how good a job you do when you make a new investment, and when you get out. We refer to these things as our Entry Efficiency and Exit Efficiency. They're some of the most important factors in your overall performance.

Hey, you finished Module 7! You're breezing through these modules like it's nothing at all. In the next module, we'll start teaching you how to generate high returns consistently over time.

Module 7 Top Tip: Technical Analysis

Technical analysis is a way of looking at price data to find clues about future price direction. Technical analysis uses statistical studies which fall into two main categories: trend following and mean reversion.

Trend following studies like moving averages looks at a series of price averages over time to determine if a trend is in place. The Moving Average Convergence Divergence or MACD is a trend indicator that shows the relationship between two moving averages of prices.

Mean reversion studies like Relative Strength Indicator tries to predict oversold or overbought market conditions.

Ultimately, prices matter and charts can help us put the current price into its historical context.

MODULE EIGHT

Strategic Success

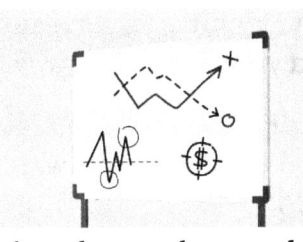

Lesson One: Develop a Game Plan

You're developing all the right habits to become a successful investor: reading the news; following the markets and the price action like a hawk; checking out the charts; chatting to family, friends, colleagues, classmates and other successful investors in private leagues or in the Invstr Feed.

Are you feeling financially fit yet?

By now, you've probably practiced buying and selling different stocks and instruments. Hopefully you're starting to get a good understanding of what kind of investor you are, what you're good at, and how you're performing compared to the community.

This means you're ready to start investing for real! But before you run off to start buying and selling, hold on a sec...

Your Investment Process

Long-term success doesn't happen by accident. We all need to take time to develop our game plan. In this module, we're going to go through the key steps in an investment game plan, or what a professional money manager would call their investment strategy.

A good investment process is essential! It's like our own manual for successful long-term investing. It takes us through the steps we need to follow and can be a handy reference guide for when things go wrong.

In this lesson, we're going to cover the first step in the game plan: defining our objectives. Sure, we all want to generate great investment returns. But your specific financial objectives will differ based on a number of factors, like your age, how much money you have, your risk appetite, and your financial targets.

Let's look at how we would begin to develop our game plan. Say you're 24 years old. You have $1000 to invest. You want to double your money by the time you're 30.

The Rule of 72

There's a simple way of working out what investment returns you need to generate each year to hit your target. It's called the Rule of 72. It states that if you want to double your money, you need to divide the number 72 by the number of years you've allowed yourself to achieve your target. The result will be the return you need to generate each year to double your money. The Rule of 72 is not exact, but it's a good approximation and useful shortcut.

For example: if you want to double your money in six years, from age 24 to 30, simply divide 72 by 6. You'll end up with 12. 12% is the return you will to generate each year to turn $1,000 into $2,000 by the time you're 30. (12% a year is approximately an average of 1% a month.)

Defining Your Objectives

Defining your objectives will help you manage your portfolio successfully over time. It'll also let you measure your success according to your game plan, and not the ups and downs of the market.

Let's say you were making 4% in a month. Without a game plan, it'd be easy to keep hoping that the market would continue going your way. However, if you have a 1% average monthly return target in your mind, you might decide to lock in some of those gains and reduce your risk. Or you might use other methods to protect your portfolio, like putting in place stop losses or limit orders (we'll discuss this in Module 9).

So, how do you go about defining your objectives?

1. Start with your age.
2. Define your time horizon—how long you want to invest for? The longer you plan for, the better.
3. Think carefully about how much money you can afford to invest now and in future months and years.
4. Think about how quickly you want to see your money grow. Be careful here! The quicker you want it to grow, the more risk you'll need to take to achieve a higher return. The more risk you take, the greater the chance that something will go wrong and you end up losing money.

Defining your objectives will also help you to manage your emotions as well as your money. Preserving your emotional capital is as important as preserving your financial capital; to maximize your returns, you want to stay calm enough to buy when prices are low (and everyone else is panicking) and sell when prices are high (and everyone else is buying).

The financial markets always give us an opportunity to make money. But it can also go the opposite way. A good game plan with clearly defined objectives will help us take advantage of those opportunities to make money consistently over the long term.

Lesson Two: Develop an Investment Strategy

You've defined your objectives: you know what you want to achieve and over what timeframe. It's the first step in your game plan. Step two is to figure out *how* you're going to do it.

Your Investment Strategy

The *how* is your investment strategy: what kind of investments are you going to make that will help you meet your investment objectives? Your investment strategy has to be consistent with your investment objectives.

For example: if your investment objectives are to make 1% a month, then you probably want to have a reasonably balanced portfolio with a small allocation to investments that can generate a slightly higher return. You wouldn't want to put all of your money into cryptocurrencies!

There are many possible investments you can choose from, including thousands of stocks, bonds, commodities, and cryptocurrencies. You could try to invest a little in all of them, or try to focus on a smaller number. As you start to develop your investment strategy, there are two things you need to take into account:

Investment Mandate

The first is to think about what you want to invest in. If you think about stocks, then there are three main decisions to make:

1. Which country or countries do you want to invest in? For example: do you want to invest in US companies or international companies? If the latter, do you want to invest in developed countries or emerging market countries?
2. Which sectors do you want to invest in? For example: the most popular sectors on Invstr have been technology, consumer, auto, and financial companies. Healthcare stocks can also be very profitable if you can find promising new companies to invest in.
3. Do you want to buy large companies or smaller companies? Over a very long period of time, smaller companies have generated higher returns than large companies. In fact, many of the largest companies today were small companies not that long ago!

We call these three things collectively (geography, sector and market capitalization) your investment mandate. The broader your investment mandate, the more diversified your portfolio is likely to be. Greater diversification means that your portfolio is less likely to suffer extreme changes in valuation— either down or up. Diversification is one of the key drivers in helping you achieve consistent returns over a longer period of time.

Characteristics of Stocks

The second thing or things to think about for an equity portfolio are the characteristics of the stocks you invest in. This will help you diversify your portfolio in another dimension. There are four main characteristics of stocks:

1. Growth stocks: companies that are generating fast growth in their sales or net profits
2. Momentum stocks: companies whose share price is moving up steadily
3. Value stocks: stocks that are cheap relative to their peer group
4. Income stocks: stocks that pay a large dividend every quarter

The combination of what instruments you invest in, your mandate, and the characteristics of those instruments, or style, will together define your investment strategy.

Developing your own investment strategy will help you focus your energy and develop your skills. But this doesn't mean that your investment strategy can't change over time! In fact, it *should* as the markets evolve. It means that you can make the job of investing better suited to who you are, what you like, and what you're good at.

Lesson Three: Develop an Investment Outlook

So far, you've defined two steps in your investment process: your objectives and your strategy. Just by doing this, you're already way ahead of most investors.

The third step in your investment process is putting that preparation to good use as you seek out opportunities in the marketplace. It's where you pause to analyze the playing field before you charge in.

Because, as we saw in Module 6, the financial markets are constantly moving and evolving. And it can be hard to keep up with everything that's going on in the world.

An Investment Outlook

Step three in your game plan is to develop an investment outlook. It's your set of expectations about the things that'll impact your investment strategy. It's about seeing the wood instead of the trees.

You can develop your investment outlook using a simple framework that helps you understand what's going on and identifies things to look out for. This framework involves asking yourself three questions:

1. What Has Happened?

Before you charge in with your investment strategy, you first need to know what kind of a market environment you're charging into. Make it a routine to ask yourself what's happening. You can do this by following certain asset classes or even the whole financial markets using the sequence we discussed in Module 6.

By following just a few instruments (the Fed Funds rate, 2 year bonds, 10 year bonds, the major FX rates like EURUSD or USDJPY, the price of oil and gold, and the major stock indexes in the US, Europe, and Asia), you can have as good a sense of what has happened in the world as many professional investors.

2. Why Has It Happened?

The second thing to understand is why it has happened. For example: if the price of oil has suddenly shot up, try to understand what caused it. It might be something obvious like a big conflict in the Middle East or it might be something more subtle. Every change in the market happens for a reason!

There are different ways to understand why things have happened. The more obvious things will be reported in the news. For less obvious events, it helps to talk to people you know or respect —and you'll probably get a variety of different views.

The more curious you are about investigating the causes of events, the better you get at forecasting what could happen next. Investing is all about the future. It's much easier to make predictions about the future if we understand the present.

3. What Might Happen Next?

Unless you're a time traveler, you'll never know for certain what's going to happen next. Even so, try to develop predictions about what might happen next. Using our example above, if you think that the price of oil is going to continue rising, you might decide to buy oil company stocks. If you think it was just a temporary blip, then you can take profits on any oil stocks you own.

Use the theories and foundations you've developed in this book as your guide to develop your investment outlook. If the markets follow your predictions, then it means your outlook is coming true! That gives you a huge advantage when it comes to executing your investment strategy. If your outlook appears wrong, go back to step 1 and start again.

Part of the fascination with investing is trying to predict the future. If you can be consistently right more often than not, you're on your way to becoming a successful investor.

Lesson Four: What Should I Buy?

It's awesome to be right about the future, but that's not enough to become a successful investor. Good investing isn't just about being right. It's about making money consistently over time.

The difference between being right and making money is choosing the best investments to make, how much, when to get in, and when to get out. These four steps are the next four steps in your game plan.

In this lesson, we're going to consider the question that most people ask when they start investing: what should I buy?

There are a few things to consider:

What Will Perform Well?

Based on what you know of the world, think about the investments in your strategy that are most likely to perform well. If you think that the price of oil is going to continue rising, AND if your strategy includes investing in oil stocks, then take a closer look at the oil stocks you like to follow.

What's the Company's Story?

As we discovered in Module 2 with Emma's lemonade business, every company has a story. Think about the story of each company on your list. If the price of oil is soaring, you'd be better investing in a company that has proven oil reserves instead of one that's still exploring for oil. If the price of oil in Europe is going up more than the price of oil in America, choose a company that sells oil in Europe.

What's the Company's Income?

Next, start to look at a company's income. For example, some oil companies lock in the price at which they sell their oil. That means that if the price of oil goes up, they don't make more money. It also means that if the price of oil falls, they don't lose money. If you're buying oil companies because you think the price of oil is going up, invest in the companies that will make more money if that happens.

What Are the Risks?

Consider the risks. Do any of the companies you're looking at have plans to sell equity? That could temporarily depress the price of their shares. Do they have environmental liabilities? Are their workers about to go on strike?

All of these considerations and others will help you choose which companies are right for you, right now.

As you go through your game plan, you'll start narrowing down the list of investments you make based on your objectives, strategy, outlook, and the specific nature of each investment. As the markets change and your view of the world changes, the choices you make will also change. The thing that will change least is your game plan. It will be your guide through your investing journey and grow more refined as you become a better investor.

Lesson Five: How Much Should I Buy?

Once you've chosen what you want to buy, there are still at least three more steps in your game plan. The next step is to decide *how much* you want to buy.

It'll be tempting to put your whole portfolio into your chosen investment. After all, you've done so much work to understand what's going on in the world, why it has happened, and what might happen next.

But as we saw previously, investing is not about being right. It's about making money. And the best way to do that is to preserve your financial and emotional capital.

How? By remaining diversified.

Diversification

Don't be tempted to put all of your eggs in one basket! When you make a new investment, make it a part of your portfolio, not your whole portfolio. A good way to do this is to set yourself guidelines. For example:

- You should have no less than 2.5% and no more than 20% of your portfolio in any one instrument. That way, you ensure that you have neither too many investments to follow nor too few to be diversified.
- You should have no more than 40% in any one sector. That way, you always have a minimum of three sectors in a fully invested portfolio and no fewer than five individual investments.
- You could also decide to rank your investments on a simple three score system: 3 for a very high conviction idea; 2 for a medium conviction idea; and 1 for a low conviction idea. If you're convinced an instrument will make you a strong return (a 3 score), you should make it a larger portion of your portfolio (versus a riskier instrument scoring a 1). A score of 3 could equate to 15% of your overall portfolio; a score of 1 should equate to 5% of your portfolio.

If you have a system for making the right sized investments, you'll know why you're making money when you're successful. Over time, you'll become a better judge of your own scoring abilities, and your investment decisions will improve as well!

Lesson Six: When Should I Buy?

Choosing what you should buy and how much you should buy are important. But *when* you should make an investment is possibly the most important decision you'll make.

In fact, bad investments executed with good timing can pay off better than good investment decisions executed with bad timing. As the saying goes, "Better lucky than smart."

For example: the price of Google rises by 12% steadily over a year, while Tesla only rises 2% over the year, but is highly volatile. Google is a much better investment over the whole year. But if you bought Google from February to March, you might only have made a 1% return. If Tesla had spiked higher between February and March, you might have been better off buying Tesla during that time period. Your investment time horizons and your timing are really important factors in your overall investment returns.

A recent study showed that most of the returns that people make are generated during small windows of time; the biggest returns tend to be right after the worst days in the market. If you weren't invested during those winning days, then you would've missed out on most of the returns of the market.

Technical Analysis

There are two ways to deal with this issue of market timing. One is to become very good at it through technical analysis and following the markets closely. You wait to buy when the momentum in the price declined, and the investment was a little cheaper than before. This is a practice that requires both patience and skill.

Averaging-in

The other way is to buy a little at a time. This practice is known as averaging-in. For example, if you decide to allocate 20% to a particular investment with very high conviction, then you might want to buy 5% now, 5% a week from now, 5% a week later, and 5% a week after that.

If the market goes up over the following three weeks, your average price will always be lower than the market price. If the price goes down over the next three weeks, your average price will be lower than if you had bought all 20% on day one.

As the saying goes, timing is everything! Even though it's step 6 of our game plan or investment process, it's still very important.

Lesson Seven: When Should I Sell?

Almost as important as knowing when to buy is knowing when to sell. There's nothing more frustrating than seeing great investment returns vanish as the market turns down, or seeing losses get larger and larger.

Luckily, there are ways to avoid both of these scenarios: by having a plan for when you're going to sell your investments.

The best time to determine when to sell is before you've bought! After you make an investment and it goes up in value, it's easy to think that you're the smartest person in the world (which might be true!). It can be even easier to get attached to an investment when it's making money.

But an investment is not part of the family, nor is it a close friend or favorite pet. An investment is not for life! There will always be a time when we need to say farewell to one of our investments.

Averaging-out

When we make a new investment, we should determine how we expect it to perform. We can set price levels at which we'll sell part or all of our stake. This is called averaging-out.

Averaging-out works just like averaging-in, but in reverse. We sell parts of the investment at different prices. By the time the price has reached the highest price we determined, we have sold out of our investment.

We should also have a plan if the investment doesn't work out so well. This includes determining the price below which our investment plan is simply wrong. We should be prepared to liquidate our investment if it's not performing well—just like subbing out bad performers on a sports team.

Planning ahead for both success and failure will help us become a great investor. Don't make up the plays as you're going along. Give your investments and your portfolio the love they deserve by having a plan and sticking to it!

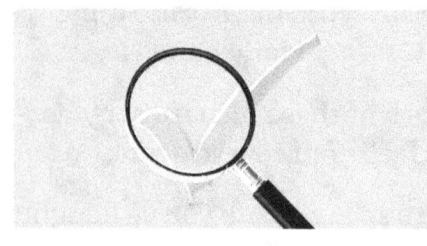

Lesson Eight: How Am I Doing?

So far, we've defined seven steps in a good game plan:

1. Being clear on what your objectives are
2. Developing an investment strategy
3. Developing an investment outlook, thinking about what could happen next
4. Choosing what investments to make
5. How much to invest
6. When to invest
7. When to get out

We call this an investment process. But there's also an eighth step in any good game plan—judging two things:

1. How good of a job did you do sticking to the plan?
2. How good of an investment process is it?

Make time for yourself to review your progress on a regular basis. Be honest. If you broke your guidelines, be clear about it. If you stuck to your plan and it didn't work, try to understand which of the steps you need to change. Are your objectives too ambitious? Are you trying to run before you can walk? Are you spending enough time thinking about the markets? Are your investment decisions good or bad?

Sometimes, it's easier to learn from our mistakes than our successes. So, cherish the investments that didn't work out, because they could be valuable lessons for the future. After all, that's what investing is about, isn't it?

Guess what?! You've completed Module 8! Only two more modules left...

Module 8 Top Tip: Remembering Stocks, Bonds, and Commodities

It's never too late to go back to the basics! In case your memory needs refreshing, here's the difference between stocks, bonds, and commodities:

Stocks are a unit of ownership in a business, representing an entitlement to the profits of that business.

Bonds are a type of borrowing in the form of a tradable security that can be bought and sold by investors. They represent one of the two main types of borrowing, alongside loans. Bonds are sold by companies or governments to investors, and are certificates of debt that promise to pay back the lender the entire principal of the bond, as well as a certain amount of interest, at the bond's date of maturity.

Commodities are fungible assets (in other words: interchangeable with other assets) and traditionally include agricultural products (soft commodities), precious and base metals and oil, and may also include financial instruments and indexes.

MODULE NINE

Brokerage Accounts

Lesson One: What is a Brokerage Account?

By now, you're probably more than ready to start investing. So how do you actually do it?

The answer is that you need to open a brokerage account. A brokerage account is where you can make and hold different investments. For most people, that means buying and selling securities that trade on regulated exchanges—stocks, bonds and Exchange Traded Funds. These accounts are overseen by brokers who execute our trades and investments for us based on what we tell them to do.

Opening a brokerage account with a broker is very straightforward. Invstr lets you do it from within the app with our partners!

In this module, I'm going to take you through everything you need to know about opening a brokerage account and investing for real. (Note that you need to be 18 years old to open a US brokerage account. If you're under 18, your parents or guardians can open an account for you.) I'll also explain why brokers have to ask you lots of questions about yourself.

We're in the home stretch! Let's get right to it.

Lesson Two: What is Know Your Customer?

Brokers are required by regulators to understand who their clients are and where their money came from. This is to prevent money from illegal activities entering the financial system.

Know Your Customer

Know your customer (KYC) are the guidelines for knowing who brokerage clients are and where their money came from. They're required by Anti-Money Laundering (AML) regulations.

Brokers are also required to ensure that clients make investments that are suitable for them. This is called Client Suitability. This means that the broker is responsible for keeping their client from investing too much money into risky investments, ensuring that they do not jeopardize their financial safety.

Opening an Account

When you open a brokerage account, you'll be asked the same questions by whichever broker you choose. The answers you provide are confidential and won't be used for any purpose other than opening an account. It should only take a few minutes (no trick questions!).

There are three types of information you'll need to provide:

1. Who you are. This includes information that helps your broker verify your identity (like your social security number if you're a US citizen and your passport number if you're a non-US citizen). This makes sure you're a real person, and are investing your own money.
2. Your personal status, including your employment status and income. This allows the broker to better understand your background, and what investments are right for you.
3. Your investment experience and objectives, and the risk you're willing to take to reach them. This helps the broker know what advice to give you, what trades to make for you, and when to decide that a trade isn't suitable for your investment strategy.

If you want to be ready, you can see the full list of questions here.

Account Registration Information
First name
Last name
Email
Password
User name

Personal Identification
Date of birth
Citizenship
Domicile

Home Address
Mobile phone number
Passport number
Social Security number

Personal status
Marital status
Employment status
Employer
Type of business
Employer country
Annual Income
Liquid Net Worth
Total Net Worth

Experience & Objectives
Investment Experience - low, medium high
Objectives - income, capital growth
Risk tolerance - low, medium, high

Control
Broker affiliation- affiliated to a broker dealer
Control person - affiliated to a company insider
PEP - affiliated to a politically exposed person

Legal Terms & Conditions
Privacy Policy
Terms & Conditions
Notifications

Lesson Three: What is Client Sustainability?

As we saw in Module 4, different investments behave in different ways. Some asset classes and sectors are riskier than others. They move up and down more.

The more money or time you have before you need to sell your investments, the more risk you can afford to take.

Assessing Client Suitability

Brokers are required by FINRA regulations to make sure that any recommendations they make to clients are suitable for the client. This prevents the client from taking on investments that are too risky, or where there's insufficient liquidity to buy or sell easily. There are a few ways of assessing if an investment is suitable for an individual client.

For example: if an investor is 25 years old and they're saving for their retirement in 40 years' time, it might be fine to own investments that could go up or down in value a lot in the short term. The expectation would be that over a longer period of time, the value of the investment will have risen more than a less risky investment.

However, an investor who's 60 years old and retiring will need to start using their investments for their daily living needs. They can't afford to make investments that could go down in value substantially. An older person's portfolio will have a higher proportion of less risky investments, such as government bonds.

Risk Tolerance

What's suitable for each investor also depends on their risk tolerance. Think of risk tolerance like crossing the road: some people will wait until a road is completely clear of traffic before crossing. They have low risk tolerance or are risk-averse.

Some people might start jay-walking across moving traffic. These people have a high-risk tolerance. You're less likely to get run over if you're risk averse. But you might get across the road quicker if you're more risk tolerant!

It's the same in investing. Some people are willing to make a risky investment and lose a great deal of that investment because they know it's worth the risk. They might also be willing to hold onto investments through a bad dip if they believe it'll begin to increase again. These investors have no problem investing in high-risk, high-reward instruments if their successes continue to outweigh their losses.

Others have a harder time stomaching large losses, and get squeamish the moment investments drop into the red. This is okay too! Those who are less risk averse will instead opt for stocks that grow steadily over time, but with potentially lower returns.

Everyone is different. There are no right or wrong answers for what we should invest in. The only thing that matters is what's right for you. Your broker will work to ensure your investments suit your personal risk tolerance and situation.

Lesson Four: How Do I Put Money into My Brokerage Account?

Once your brokerage account has been approved, the next thing you need to do is put money into it. This is called funding your account.

Fund your account right away so you can start putting your investment skills to work! It's easy: if you have a US bank account, you can link that account to your brokerage account. Once you do that, you can move money from your bank account to your brokerage account quickly and cheaply.

If you don't have a US bank account, there are other ways to get money into your brokerage account on Invstr:

Wire transfer: A wire transfer is when you send money from a foreign bank account. It usually takes one or two days for the money to reach your account. Your bank will also charge you a fee for doing this.

Debit/credit card: This will take one or two days, and will cost you 2-4% of the amount you're transferring.

Other services: Sometimes, brokers allow you to use other services like PayPal or TransferWise to transfer money into your brokerage account.

There are lots of options out there. Whatever service you use, be sure to check how long it'll take and cost you!

Lesson Five: Is My Money Safe?

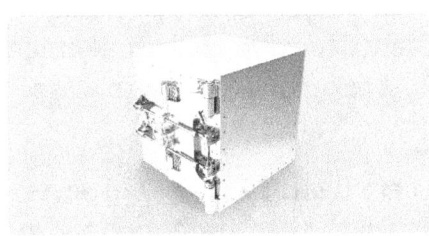

When you transfer money to someone else, you might worry about whether or not that money is safe. It's a totally valid fear, and good that you're already thinking about safety and security.

When it comes to investing in US securities, there are a few things that should help you sleep better at night:

Regulation

All legitimate US broker dealers are regulated. As we saw in Module 5, the main securities regulators are the SEC (Securities & Exchange Commission) and FINRA (Financial Industry Regulatory Authority).

FINRA is the self-regulatory organization (SRO) that regulates the brokerage industry. FINRA's job is to make sure that:

- The people who are running brokers know what they're doing
- The proper procedures are in place for managing their

clients' money
- Every broker has enough of its own money (or capital) to reduce the risk of going out of business

Always check that your broker is licensed with FINRA. You can verify that your broker is properly regulated here: https://brokercheck.finra.org/

(When you open a brokerage account on Invstr, your account is regulated by the SEC and FINRA.)

Protection

If a broker does go out of business, the Securities Investor Protection Corporation (SIPC) steps in. The SIPC was created by Congress to protect the money clients have in their brokerage account from the bankruptcy of the broker. It's like having a second line of defense.

The SIPC insures up to $500,000 per client: $250,000 in securities, and up to another $250,000 in cash that's intended for investment purposes.

It's important to remember that the SIPC is different from the Federal Deposit Insurance Corporation (FDIC). The FDIC protects money held in bank accounts, while the SIPC only protects money held in brokerage accounts from a broker's bankruptcy. It does not protect your investments from going down in value—that's your job!

Lesson Six: How Does the Broker Make Money?

Brokers are businesses, and they make money from you! They charge you a fee every time you buy or sell an investment. This fee is called an execution or trading commission. A broker might also charge you fees for making sure the investments you buy are properly delivered to your account, and for looking after your investments. These services are called clearing and custody fees.

There are other ways brokers can make money. Let's say a broker had two clients. One wanted to buy a stock. The other wanted to sell the same stock. If this happened at the same time, the broker could take the stock from the client who wanted to sell and pass it to the client who wanted to buy. Their profit would be the difference between the buying and selling price, or trading spread.

Market Makers

Not every broker has clients who want to buy and sell the same stock at the same time. Instead of profiting from the trading spread themselves, brokers pass all of their clients' requests to people who specialize in doing this.

As we saw in Module 5, these people are called market makers. The market makers make money between the buying and selling price. They pass a fee or kick-back to the broker who brought them the business.

Transparency

Brokers have a regulatory obligation to be transparent with you about their charges. They're also required by the NBBO to ensure that you get the best price when you buy or sell something.

But beware of brokers who tell you they're not charging you for your business. Someone is always making money from you! If your broker is passing all of your business to market makers with large spreads, it could actually be more expensive for you to be trading for free vs. paying a trading commission!

Another way brokers can make money from you is by earning interest on the cash you keep in your brokerage account. Some brokers will pay you a rate of interest on your cash. Others may not. Brokers can also earn money by lending your stock to someone who wants to borrow it to make a short trade.

Nothing in business is free! A business makes money by providing a service to its clients. Brokers are businesses, not charities. If it's too good to be true, then it probably isn't true.

Lesson Seven: How Do I Buy or Sell Securities?

You've opened your account. You've put money in it. You've found something you want to buy. You've figured out how much you should buy and when you should buy it.

You're ready to make an investment! It's time to tell your broker what you want to do.

Communicating with your broker is called giving them an order. These days, you don't need to pick up the phone or even send your broker an email! On a mobile app or website, orders are placed electronically.

The order will state which stock you want to buy or sell, how much you want to buy, and at what price. An order will also tell the broker when you want the order to be executed.

Types of Orders

There are different types of orders that achieve all of these things. The most common type is a Market Order. The market order tells the broker to buy or sell an amount of stock at the current market price. These orders are usually executed immediately. If the market is closed when you place the order, it's executed once the market opens, usually within the first ten minutes of the day.

When you ran through your investment strategy, you also decided at what price you want to sell each investment you make. There are two types of orders that do this: a stop-loss order tells the broker to sell the investment if the price falls below a certain level. A limit order tells the broker to sell the investment if the price reaches a certain level.

You can also place a limit order before you've bought a stock. For example, you could tell your broker to buy a stock priced at $1000 when it falls to $950.

Some brokers will accept Good 'til Canceled (GTC) orders. These tell the broker to keep managing the order beyond today until you change your mind and cancel the order. That way, you can rest knowing what your maximum loss is likely to be.

Fractional Trading

What if you don't have enough money to buy one share in a company's stock? Buying one share each in the FAANGs (Facebook, Apple, Amazon, Netflix and Google) would cost over $3,500 today. Just buying one share of the cheapest FAANG would cost at least $150!

The problem is that we know being diversified is an essential part of being a good investor. But how can we diversify our portfolios if the stocks we want are so expensive? This is where fractional trading can be very useful.

Fractional trading allows us to specify the amount of money we want to invest in a stock, rather than the number of shares we want to buy. That way, we can start investing with smaller amounts of money in each company while still being diversified.

You can give fractional trading orders on Invstr. It's the perfect way to start investing, especially if you don't want to buy full shares yet!

Lesson Eight: How Do I Know I'm Getting a Good Price?

We've seen that prices in financial markets are constantly changing. In fact, they can change many times a second. It's important to make sure that we pay the right price for our investments when we place our orders.

Regulators in the US require all brokers to execute client trades at the national best bid or offer (NBBO) prevailing at the time of the trade. This rule is called Best Execution. It ensures that clients obtain the most competitive prices when buying or selling stocks.

If you want to buy a stock, you'll get the National Best Offer. If you want to sell a stock, you'll get the National Best Bid. The difference between these two prices is called the Bid-Offer spread. When you trade with a zero-commission broker, you're likely to get either the bid or the offer price. When you trade with a commission broker, you might be able to achieve a price that's between the bid and offer price.

Lesson Nine: How Do I Find the Value of My Portfolio?

As you make investments through your broker, you slowly start to build up your portfolio. Your portfolio is the sum of all the investments you have made. It also includes any cash you have not yet invested.

Every investment in your portfolio constitutes a position. Each position represents the amount of money you have invested in a stock and the number of whole or fractional shares you own in the stock.

The prices of most currencies, cryptocurrencies, stocks, commodities, and bonds all change in value on a frequent basis. Some investments, like real estate, wine, or classic cars, may change in price much less frequently.

Each of your positions is constantly revalued to the current market price. This process is called marking to market. The only thing that's not revalued is your cash. As each of your positions is revalued, the value of your overall portfolio also changes. On Invstr, we show you the value of your portfolio as it changes second to second, and also the returns you've made on each position.

When a bond pays a coupon or a stock pays a dividend, the value of that coupon or dividend is usually added to your portfolio in the form of cash. This increases the amount of money you have available to invest.

Corporate Actions

The process of marking to market and collecting coupons and dividends is done automatically by your broker. Other things could affect the investments in your portfolio:

- Two companies might merge
- One company could acquire another company
- A company could split its shares by exchanging each share with two. This is called a stock-split. Stock splits don't change the value, or market capitalization, of a company. Instead, they merely change how many shares the value of the company is divided into.
- A company could take back two of its shares and re-issue just one. This is called a reverse-split.

Together all of these things are called corporate actions.

Your portfolio is constantly changing. Hopefully, it's steadily going up in value. Even so, be sure to show it some love and attention on a regular basis.

Lesson Ten: Reporting and Tax

When it comes to investing, we have some good news and bad news. The good news is that you made money! The bad news is that the government usually wants to collect part of that money from you in the form of tax.

There are two kinds of taxes that you may have to pay. You'll have to pay an income tax on any dividends or coupons you receive from your investments. In addition, you'll pay a capital gains tax whenever you sell an investment and make a gain. The capital gain is the same as the profit you made on your investment from the time you bought it to the time you sold it.

Your broker provides transaction and tax reporting to help you keep track of your performance. It also helps you comply with the legal obligations of reporting your income, gains, and losses to the tax authorities. They'll send you a statement that details any income and capital gains you have realized on your account.

You'll need to add these to your tax return, along with other income and capital gains. If you've suffered other realized losses, these can usually be offset against your realized profits. If in doubt, get professional tax advice.

Always remember to include any gains on cryptocurrencies. These must also be reported just like any other investment.

We've come to the end of Module 9! Can you believe it? You're just one module away from finishing this book!

Module 9 Top Tip: Types of Orders

There are different types of orders that achieve all of these things. The most common type is a market order. The market order tells the broker to buy or sell an amount of stock at the current market price. These orders are usually executed immediately. If the market is closed when you place the order, it's executed once the market opens, usually within the first ten minutes of the day.

A stop-loss order tells the broker to buy or sell a security when it reaches a defined price.

A limit order tells a broker to buy or sell a security at a specific price or better.

You can also place a limit order before you've bought a stock. For example, you could tell your broker to buy a stock priced at $1000 when it falls to $950.

Some brokers will accept Good 'til Canceled (GTC) orders. These tell the broker to keep managing the order beyond today until you change your mind and cancel the order. That way, you can rest knowing what your maximum loss is likely to be.

MODULE TEN

Top Tips

Lesson One: Manage Your Emotional Capital

There's a big difference between playing and learning, and investing for real. That difference is you!

Successful investing is as much about managing ourselves as it is about managing our money. When real money is involved and we have large profits or losses in our portfolio, it's easy for our emotions to take over and for us to make bad decisions.

To help prevent this, evaluate every position in your portfolio with a fresh pair of eyes. If you didn't already own it, would you buy it, sell it, or do nothing? Only hold positions where you have positive belief in your investment. If in doubt, get out! You can always get back in another day.

Being objective and basing your decisions on what the market is telling you will help preserve your emotional capital. Staying emotionally strong will help you to maximize your financial capital over the long run.

Investing is about your future and you. *You* are the key to your success. The better you are at managing yourself, the more successful you'll be as an investor.

Lesson Two: Plan for Success

It's a lot easier to aim when we have a target to aim at. Having clearly defined objectives and goals helps us manage both our successes and failures. It also helps us cut losses and take profits when we're straying too far from our targets.

Set yourself an ambitious but realistic target for your investment portfolio. This could be a return of 5-15% per annum, depending on your circumstances. When you're making more money than expected, take some profits. When you're performing poorly, reduce your risk.

Failing to plan is planning to fail. Understanding yourself, your budget, objectives, and what you want from your portfolio should form the basis of all your investment decisions. Every instrument you add to your portfolio should serve a specific purpose and fit within the overarching strategy you laid out for your future.

Lesson Three: Build Stamina for Long-Term Returns

Investing is a marathon, not a sprint. The longer you can stay in the race, the more you'll benefit from the compounding returns on your portfolio. You need all the stamina you can get!

Diversification is the key to building your investment stamina. The more you diversify your portfolio, the less you'll leave yourself exposed to the adverse movement of one instrument.

Markets don't move up in straight lines. They move up and down to shake off weak investors before moving up again. If you're too exposed to any one investment, you won't be able to withstand the downs. You'll be forced to cut your losses before the market moves up again.

Calibrate how much you invest in each investment according to its volatility. If you can have more stamina than the market (as in, if you can hold on when others are giving up), then you can ride the ups and downs of the market in comfort.

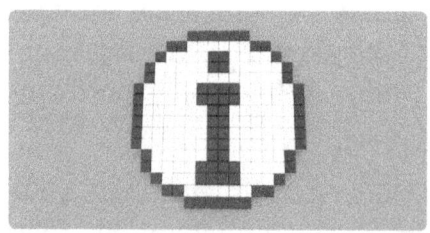

Lesson Four: Make Informed Decisions

Do your homework before you invest! That means gathering as much information as you can before you risk your money. Take the time to develop your own sources of information and refer to them on a regular basis.

The more you understand the markets, the better your portfolio will perform. Following global and industry trends, and researching company or instrument-specific information is the best way to ensure you're choosing the right investments.

If you're unsure what's going on, do more research. Read the news, talk to people, follow the price action, and look at the charts. If in doubt, stay out. A fool and his (or her!) money are easily parted. Be the smartest investor you can be.

Invstr is designed to be a useful companion to the markets. Play, learn, and share with others before you invest for real.

Lesson Five: Make Peripheral Vision Your Investment Superpower

Great athletes have great peripheral vision. They see what's happening on the field of play better than others. It helps them anticipate moves and be one step ahead of their opponents.

Like a good sportsman, your most powerful investment sense is your peripheral vision. Look out for trends in other asset classes, industries, and companies to prevent you from being blindsided. Different markets may offer clues to things that might affect your portfolio.

Peripheral vision will also bring you more investment opportunities. The wider you look, the more opportunities you'll find. Start out by building your investment skills in what you know. As you develop your confidence, start exploring other companies, sectors, or asset classes.

Ultimately, your peripheral vision will improve what you do already and help you find ways to increase your returns.

Lesson Six: Be Methodical

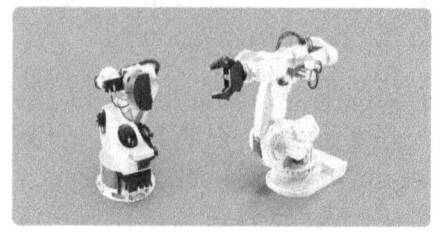

Develop a methodology for analyzing information. Use it consistently to strengthen your investing process.

You might prefer to start "top-down" by looking at the bigger picture and using your worldly wisdom to analyze what's happening. Or, you might prefer to start "bottom-up" and research individual stocks first.

Always ask yourself: what has happened, why did it happen, what might happen next?

Using a systematic and consistent approach to analyze markets allows you to tune out the noise of the markets and stay in line with your strategy.

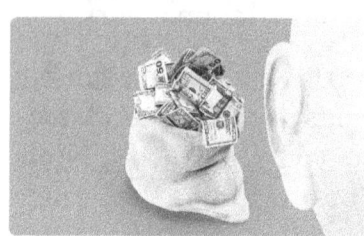

Lesson Seven: Listen to the Markets

The market is always right. Once you develop an outlook for what you expect to happen, test it out in the marketplace. You can do this in a fantasy portfolio or you can do it for real with a small amount of money.

It helps to write down your outlook. Not just so you can remember it, but to keep yourself honest! We all tend to have selective memories. Your outlook should have clear propositions: what it is that you expect to happen; the reasons why you think it'll happen; what impact it'll have on the prices of your investments.

If things are happening as you predicted, it's likely that your outlook is correct. If the market tells you your outlook is wrong, or even if prices move where you expected but for different reasons, then re-evaluate your outlook.

The more dispassionate you can be, the more you'll learn to listen to the signals coming from the market. Listening and learning will help you adapt your investment strategy as the markets evolve.

Lesson Eight: A Little Timing Makes a Big Difference

Successful investing is about making money. It's not about being right. Choosing the right investment to make is important. Buying it at the right price is almost just as important.

You can use charts to help you pick the right time and price to buy. Longer time-frames allow you to see the long-term trend. The trend is always your friend! Make investments in line with the trend.

Going from longer to shorter time frames will allow you to invest in line with the long-term trend and use shorter-term time frames to time your entry and exit levels.

Buying when the price is low and selling when the price is high will help you make money consistently. Buying an instrument at too high a price can turn a good investment decision into a bad one.

Averaging-in to positions is a useful alternative to getting your timing spot on.

Lesson Nine: Be the Boss of Your Portfolio

You should always feel like

you're in charge of your investment portfolio. You choose what goes in, you choose what stays in, and you choose what comes out.

Once you've made an investment, continue to manage it actively. If it doesn't perform the way you expect, make a conscious decision to reduce it or get out altogether.

The more you take charge of your portfolio, the more confident you'll feel. If you ever find yourself hoping for an investment to turn in your favor, it means your investment is now controlling you. Hope has no place in managing a portfolio. Once you lose control, it's time to get out.

Always be the manager of your portfolio. It's called investment management for a reason!

Lesson Ten: Never Stop Learning

Learn from everything you do - whether it's your successes or mistakes. One of the most important lessons to learn is how you behave in different situations.

Did you gather the information you needed? Did you analyze it methodically? Did you choose the right investment? Did you buy the right amount? Did you buy it at the right price? Did you sell it at the right price?

Everything you learned here is just a guide to help you become a great investor. Let it be just the start of your learning journey! Most of your learning will come through time and experience.

Investing is about your future. It's about our future. The more we invest, the better we get at it, and the better a future we can all have.

Guess what?! We've officially reached the end of the book! You've now learned everything you need to know in order to start your investing journey.

Remember, the journey doesn't end here. Keep learning, keep practicing, and most of all, have fun. Thank you for sticking with it all the way until the end. Now get out there and get investing!

Module 10 Top Tip: Diversification is Key

Remember, diversification is the key to building your investment stamina. Diversification is a strategy for lowering portfolio risk by spreading investment over several different asset classes, decreasing the potential losses following market downturns for individual asset classes.

The more you diversify your portfolio, the less you'll leave yourself exposed to the adverse movement of one instrument.

GLOSSARY

2-Factor Authentication (2FA)

An extra layer of security that adds onto the basic username and password credentials by also requiring something that only the user has on them. This is usually a piece of information only the user should know, like a personal fact or a code on a physical token.

51% Attack

A situation in which more than half of the computing power on a network is operated by a single individual or concentrated group, giving them complete control over a network. An entity with 51% of the computing power can do things such as halting all mining, halting and manipulating all interpersonal transactions, and using singular coins repeatedly for transactions.

Accredited Investor

A sophisticated investor with special status under financial regulations that allows them to invest in securities unregulated by financial authorities. Accredited investors include high net worth individuals (HNWI), banks, insurance companies, brokers, and trusts.

Active Fund

A fund overseen by a manager, who actively makes decisions about how to invest the fund's money. Conversely, a passively managed fund simply invests in line with a market index.

Active Management

An investment style involving trading securities to take advantage of market opportunities when they arise, relying on news events, research, forecasts, and more. This is in contrast to passive management.

Actuals

Physical commodities, such as oil, corn, or wheat. These commodities are traded on exchanges using derivatives and futures.

Adam Smith

Considered the father of modern capitalism and the division of labor, Adam Smith was an eighteenth-century Scottish economist, philosopher, and author. His most famous publication is the Wealth of Nations.

Aftermarket

The buying and selling of stocks and bonds after they have been first issued. It is also known as the Secondary Market.

Aggregate Risk

An FX investor's total exposure to risk based on potential fluctuations in currency value. If the investor does not have a diverse portfolio, and has invested heavily in only one currency, a fall in the value of this currency will lead to the portfolio value dropping. As such, this investor has high aggregate risk.

Aggressive

An investment approach that takes on higher levels of risk in exchange for a potentially higher rate of return.

Aggressive Growth Fund

A growth fund that seeks to invest in growth stocks that have an above average risk in return for potentially higher gains. If successful, this can result in a rate of return that is much higher than average, even for a growth fund.

Agricultural Products

Agricultural products that are grown such as coffee, cocoa, sugar, corn, wheat, soybean, fruit, and livestock.

Algo Trading

A system of trading which facilitates investment decision making using advanced mathematical tools.

Alpha

A measurement of an investment's performance compared to a benchmark index, such as the FTSE or S&P. If an investment's alpha is 3, it performed 3% better than the benchmark index.

Altcoin

The community-accepted term for any coin other than Bitcoin.

American Depository Receipts (ADR)

Certificates of foreign stocks traded on a US exchange in US dollars. ADRs represent one or more shares in a foreign company that can then be sold on exchanges in the US. Similarly, US stocks may be traded in foreign markets in that country's currency using GDRs.

Amortization

A method of repaying a debt over time. Over the life of a loan, the borrower reduces their debt through regular payments of loan installments until the loan is fully repaid.

Analyst-Research Analyst

A person who studies a certain market sector and offers investment recommendations on securities, such as 'buy' or 'sell'. In addition, analysts will often produce earnings estimates for companies in that sector.

Analyst Recommendation

An evaluation provided by analysts typically recommending whether investors should Sell, Hold or Buy a stock.

Annual General Meeting (AGM)

A company's shareholders meeting, usually held at the end of each fiscal year, to discuss the state of the company, including the previous performance of the company and the company's outlook for the future. In addition, shareholders vote on issues such as appointments to the company's board of directors, executive compensation, dividend payments, and the selection of auditors.

Annual Rate of Return

The yearly rate at which an investment gains or loses value.

Anti-Money Laundering (AML)

The process used especially by financial institutions to detect, prevent and report money laundering activities.

Appreciation

An increase in the value of an investment. It can also refer to an increase in the value of a currency in comparison to other currencies, which makes that currency more expensive to buy in FX markets.

Arbitrage

A risk-free method of trading that allows a trader to take advantage of a difference in prices between markets. The trader buys an asset in the lower-price market and simultaneously sells it in the higher-price market, thus making a profit off of the difference in price.

Article of Association

A document which, along with the memorandum of association, forms a company's constitution as well as the responsibilities of its directors.

Asset Allocation

The process of diversifying one's investments along various asset classes. This diversification limits the investor's risk and increases opportunities for generating stable returns on a portfolio.

Asset Backed Security (ABS)

Bonds or notes backed by financial assets. They consist of receivables other than mortgage loans (see Mortgage Backed Securities) such as credit card receivables, car loans, and home-equity loans.

Asset Class

A grouping of similar financial instruments. There are five popular asset classes: Foreign Exchange, Bonds, Equities, Commodities, and Cryptocurrencies. In addition, some instruments are classified in 'minor' or 'alternative' asset classes, including Private Equity, Real Estate, and Hedge Funds.

Asset Management (Asset Manager)

The management of investments on behalf of a client, with the aim of growing the client's portfolio while mitigating risk. It is a service that caters for high net-worth individuals, government entities, corporations, and financial intermediaries.

Asset Token

Tokens that represent an actual asset or product, like a token that allows for car sharing.

Asset-Backed Coin

Any cryptocurrency for which the price is pegged to a real-world asset. For example, Tether is a coin pegged to the US dollar.

Assets

Items a company owns that can add value to the company. Cash investments, inventory, office equipment, and company-owned vehicles are all examples of assets.

Average Annual Total Return

The average yearly returns from an investment or a portfolio. This includes the rise or fall in the value of an investment, dividends, and other income received.

Averaging In

Buying securities a little at a time so that if the price goes up, the average price paid will still be lower than the market price. If the price falls, the price paid will be lower than if bought as a lump sum.

Averaging Out

Selling out of an investment a little at a time as the price rises. This is an alternative strategy to selling all of an investment in a single go at a single price. It is a profit taking strategy designed to reduce risk gradually as the price rises and to achieve a better average exit price than trying to pick the top of the market.

Bagholder

Someone still holding an altcoin after a pump and dump crash. May also refer, more generally, to someone holding a coin that is sinking in value with little future prospect of recovering.

Balance Sheet

A financial statement that lists a company's assets (what it owns) and liabilities (what it owes) on any given date. The difference between a company's assets and debts is termed its net worth or shareholder's equity. Net worth is reflected on the liability side of the Balance Sheet.

Balanced Fund

A mutual fund that invests in a diversified portfolio either across asset classes or within an asset class.

Bank

A regulated financial entity that is authorized to accept money deposits from the public and then lends this money as loans to those who require funds. A bank typically earns money by paying a lower interest rate to depositors, and then lending that money to borrowers at a higher interest rate.

Bankruptcy

A legal process involving the liquidation of a business that is in financial distress, usually because it has accumulated more debt than it can repay.

Base Currency

The currency against which exchange rates are generally quoted in a given country. For example, with USD/CAD, the US Dollar is the base currency.

Base Metal

As opposed to precious metals, an inexpensive and common material such as copper, zinc, tin, lead, nickel, and aluminum.

Base Rate

The interest rate set by the Bank of England for bank-to-bank lending. The Bank of England Base Rate acts as a benchmark for other banks to lend to each other.

Basis Point (BPs)

A unit of measure equivalent to 1/100th of a percent, or 0.0001.

Bear

An adjective used to describe a downward-trending market. A bear market is usually defined as a fall of more than 20% from the recent highs of the market. A fall of less than 20% is called a correction. This is based on the direction of a bear's head, which is often held downwards, as compared to a bull whose horns point up. 'Bear' can also be used to describe an investor who is pessimistic about the market. If an investor believes the stock market will fall, he is called a 'market bear' or described as 'bearish'.

Benchmark

A standard against which an investment's rate of return or performance is measured. A benchmark is usually an index of instruments in the same asset class.

Best Execution

A duty that requires a broker to execute a trade order on behalf of the client at the best execution price possible. If the client is buying, he is entitled to buy at the best available offered price. If he is selling, he is entitled to receive the best available bid price.

Beta

A measure of an investment's volatility or risk in comparison to a benchmark index.

Bid

The price at which someone is willing to buy a security.

Bid & Ask (Bid, Ask, Offer)

The difference between the prices quoted for the buying or selling of a security, also known as Bid and Offer.

Bid Tick

The smallest amount by which a bid price can move up or down in value.

Big Mac Index

An informal method of comparing the purchasing power of currencies across the globe based on the price of a Big Mac in each country. This index was first created by *The Economist* in the 1980s.

Bitcoin

A digital payment currency that utilizes blockchain and peer-to-peer technology to create and manage monetary transactions.

Block

Files where data pertaining to the cryptocurrency network are permanently recorded. A block is like a page of a ledger or record book.

Block Reward

The reward for mining a block. The reward for mining a Bitcoin block is 25 bitcoins per block mined, which will halve after every additional 210,000 blocks are mined.

Blockchain

A blockchain is a data system that allows for the creation of a digital ledger of transactions on a non-centralized network. This means that people and computers all over the world work together to create a network, instead of the entire network being made and operated by one single person or company. This network is enabled and protected through cryptography. The blockchain is comprised of "blocks" and is constantly growing as each new record, datum, or block is added onto the chain for everyone to see.

Blocked Currency

A currency not traded on the FX market due to foreign exchange restrictions or controls.

Blue Chip

A 'safe', lower-risk stock offered by a company that is known to be reputable and financially stable. Many of these blue chips are included in major world indices, such as the FTSE and S&P.

Bollinger Band

A technical analysis tool that charts the magnitude of an instrument's volatility.

Bond Yield

The total return that an investor will receive by investing in a fixed income bond calculated from both the current price of the bond and its coupon.

Bondholder

Someone who owns a debt security, or bond, typically issued by a company or government.

Bonds

A type of borrowing in the form of a tradable security that can be bought and sold by investors. One of the two main types of borrowing, alongside loans. Bonds are sold by companies or governments to investors, and are certificates of debt that promise to pay back the lender the entire principal of the bond, as well as a certain amount of interest, at the bond's date of maturity.

Bonus Issue

The issue of new shares to current shareholders for free, often instead of a dividend.

Borrowing (Borrower)

Taking on a debt that will need to be paid back at a later date. Usually, borrowers must pay interest to their creditors, meaning that they have to pay back more than they originally borrowed.

There are two main types of borrowing: loans and bonds.

Bottom Fishing

An investment strategy that seeks to time the lows in an asset or market in the expectation that market conditions will improve and the asset or market will gain in price.

Bottom Line

A company's net profit after subtracting taxes, interest, and depreciation from net revenues. Also known as net income.

Bottom Up

An investment strategy based on in-depth knowledge about individual companies.

Box Spread

An investment strategy involving buying and selling related assets in a set ratio, ensuring all investments are hedged to reduce risk.

Broker (Stockbroker)

An intermediary who performs transactions in the marketplace on behalf of investors. The broker will buy or sell securities in exchange for a broking fee or commission, which is typically charged on each transaction.

Broker Commission (Trading commission)

A fee paid to a broker for executing a buy or sell order. Commissions are traditionally deducted from the money you invest. However, zero commission broker services take their money from the spread between the bid and ask price they quote.

Brokerage

A regulated business that offers broker or stockbroker services to its clients.

Brokerage Account

A kind of taxable investment account for depositing money with a broker for the purpose of trading in securities.

Budget

An estimate of income and expenditure over a given period.

Buffer stock

A supply of a commodity, usually held by a government, that is held in reserve. This reserve is used to guard against unforeseen changes in market demand, and can be deployed to stabilize prices during periods of high demand by selling off a portion of the reserve.

Bull

An adjective used to describe an upward-trending market. For example, if the S&P is trending upwards, it would be called a 'bull market' or described as 'bullish'. This is based on the direction of a bull's head, which is often held upwards, as compared to a bear. 'Bull' can also be used to describe an investor who is optimistic about the market. If an investor believes the S&P will continue to rise, he is called a 'market bull' or described as 'bullish'.

Bullet Bond or Loan

A type of bond which is repaid in full on the maturity date, instead of being repaid over the term of the bond.

Business

An economic player that sells a good and/or service to clients. Along with governments and households, businesses are one of the three main players in the economy, and drive much of an economy's growth.

Business Cycle

A business cycle, also known as an economic cycle, represents the recurring rise and fall of business activity in an economy, as measured by the change in growth in gross domestic product.

Business Plan

A strategy document that explains how a business plans to achieve its goals. A business plan is important, as it shows potential investors how the business expects to grow and the resources it needs to do so.

Buy Side

The financial institutions that buy investment services and assets, including private equity firms, mutual funds, life insurance companies, unit trusts, hedge funds, and pension funds.

Buy the Rumor, Sell the Fact

When a stock price moves in the opposite direction to what would normally be expected, because the market already anticipated the price move.

Buyback (Share Buyback)

A process by which a company repurchases its shares in the marketplace. This is an alternative method of returning cash to shareholders other than paying a dividend. It also enables companies to keep their share price up.

Call Option

A financial contract that gives an option buyer the right, but not the obligation, to buy a security at a specified price within a specific time period.

Capital

The total amount of money a company raises by issuing securities to equity shareholders and debt to bondholders. Capital is used to finance the machinery, factories, inventory, and financial assets a business needs to produce its products.

Capital Gain

The profit made on the sale of an asset. It is the difference between the purchase price and net sale price.

Capital Gains Tax

A tax on any profits that come from the sale of property or an investment.

Capital Inflows

The amount of capital coming into a country. For example, in the form of foreign investment.

Capital Loss

The loss made on the sale of an asset, because its net sale price was greater than its original purchase price.

Capital Markets

The primary market where companies seeking funding sell equities and bonds to investors.

Capital Surplus

Also called share premium, appears on a company's balance sheet as the amount the corporation raises on the issue of shares in excess of their nominal value.

Capitalization

The value placed by investors on a company. It is calculated by multiplying its share price by the number of shares outstanding. It indicates the size of the company, as well as how much investors believe the company is worth overall.

Capitulation

A market phenomenon in which a large wave of investors who

are disappointed in a security's losses sell their holdings of the security at the same time, causing the market price to plummet further.

Carry Trade

A trading strategy that involves borrowing at a low interest rate and investing in an asset that provides a higher rate of return.

Carrying Broker

A broker firm that provides back office functions, such as clearing, settlement, and custodial services to other brokers.

Cash Flow

The income a company is left with after accounting for tax, depreciation, depletion, amortization, and dividend payments.

Central Bank (Central banker)

A national bank that provides financial and banking services for its country's government and commercial banking system. It also implements the government's monetary policy and oversees the issuing of money.

Centralized Validation

A method of overseeing transactions in which one central authority controls every valid transaction that is happening in a network.

Certificates of Deposit (CD)

A certificate given to a person who has deposited money in a bank for a set period of time. The CD guarantees that person to receive their deposit back at a later date, plus interest.

Charting (Technical Charting, Chart)

The process of analyzing historical graphs and data in order to gather information about potential investments.

Chicago Board Options Exchange (CBOE)

The world's largest options market with contracts focusing on individual equities, indexes and interest rates. Based in Chicago, it is also the main source of real time prices on Invstr.

Clean Price

A bond price that excludes all the interest accrued since the coupon payment.

Clearing

A process whereby investment trades are settled by ensuring moneys and securities are appropriately transferred.

Client

Someone who buys a business's product, which is either a good or a service. Without clients, a business could never exist - it would have no one to sell to!

Client Suitability (suitable, suitability)

When an investment company or broker offers advice, it is responsible for ensuring its investment recommendation is suitable for the needs of the investor, based on their profile information.

Closed End Fund

An investment company that does not continually offer new shares for sale. It only sells a fixed number of shares at its initial public offering.

Closing Price

The price of a security at the end of the trading day, when the stock exchange closes.

Cold Storage

Storing digital currency offline to protect the investor from attackers or the collapse of a digital currency system.

Collateral

An asset that is used as a safeguard against a possible default on a debt or loan. For
instance, your house can be used as collateral against a business loan.

Collateralized Debt Obligation (CDO)

A type of asset-backed security, which is backed by repackaged high-risk subprime mortgage debt. Its invention, and subsequent popularity, is considered one of the causes of the 2007 financial crisis.

Command Economy

Where a central government makes all economic decisions. Also known as a Planned Economy.

Commercial Bank

A bank providing financial services to the general public. This is in contrast to investment banks, which provide financial services to companies, governments and very wealthy individuals.

Commodities (Commodity)

Fungible assets (in other words interchangeable with other assets) and traditionally include agricultural products (soft commodities), precious and base metals and oil, and may also include financial instruments and indexes.

Commodity Futures Trading Commission (CFTC)

An independent agency of the US government that regulates the futures and options markets.

Common Stock

Shares in a company that fall below preferred stocks in the share hierarchy. Also known as ordinary stock.

Company (Companies)

An economic player that sells a good and/or service to clients. Along with governments and households, businesses are one of the three main players in the economy, and drive much of an economy's growth.

Company Insider

A director of a company, or any person or entity that beneficially owns more than 10% of a company's voting shares.

Composite

A collection of equities or other securities that are averaged together to represent an overall market or sector performance, or benchmark, or index.

Compound Interest

Interest earned not only on the original investment, the principal, but also on the accumulated interest earned, or interest on interest.

Consensus Estimate

A value based on the combined estimates of analysts tracking a company. Typically, analysts offer a consensus for a company's earnings per share (EPS) and revenue.

Consumer Confidence Index (CCI)

An index that measures how optimistic or pessimistic consumers are about the economic performance in the near future.

Consumer Price Index (CPI)

A measure of inflation found by looking at how the current purchasing power of consumers compares with the past.

Contango

A situation in which the price of commodity futures that are closer to expiry are trading at lower prices than futures with longer maturity dates.

Contingent Liability Transaction (CLT)

A transaction that factors in the risk of a potential liability occurring, depending on the outcome of an uncertain future event.

Convergence

A phenomenon in which two assets or indexes move towards the same value from different directions.

Convexity

A measure of the relationship of bond prices to changes in interest rates.

Corporate Actions

An event initiated by a listed company that will bring a change to its shares. A corporate action can be a: stock split, bonus issue, spin-off, dividend payout, return of capital, rights issue, buyback offer, or a delisting, among others.

Corporate Bond

A bond issued by a business seeking to raise money.

Corporate Raider

An investor who makes hostile takeover bids for companies, either to change how they are run or to resell them for a profit.

Corporate Tax

A tax imposed on the net income of the company.

Correction

A major but temporary change in the market price of an instrument. Corrections are at least a 10% change in the opposite direction of the price change trend.

Correlation

A measure of how close the average rate of return of an instrument is to the average rate of return for an overall index.

Cost of Capital

The cost to a business of raising capital through debt and equity. When considering new projects, a company must analyze if the returns it generates from the project will outweigh the cost of capital to fund that project.

Costs

The money a business must pay to operate and sell its product to clients. These costs are subtracted from revenues to find profit.

Counter (Cyclical Stock)

A stock that outperforms during an economic downturn or recession. Conversely, they will underperform in times of economic growth.

Counterparty

An opposite party in a contract or financial transaction.

Coupon

The annual interest rate paid on a bond, expressed as percentage of the bond's face value.

Covariance

A statistical measure of the movements of two assets in relation to each other.

Crack Spread

An investment strategy in which an investor simultaneously buys oil futures and sells a derivative such as gasoline or heating oil futures to hedge against risk.

Credit (CR)

Borrowing or taking on a debt that will need to be paid back at a later date. Usually, borrowers must pay interest to their creditors, meaning that they have to pay back more than they originally borrowed. There are two main types of borrowing: loans and bonds.

Credit Crunch

A severe shortage of money or credit available to borrow, often due to a financial crisis.

Credit Default Swaps (CDS)

A swap contract in which a lender, who is worried about a borrower defaulting, buys a CDS from another party, who in exchange promises to cover the lender's losses in the case of default.

Credit Quality

The creditworthiness of a bond or debt issue. In other words, the evaluation of a debtor's ability to pay back the debt.

Credit Rating

A measure of a borrower's risk of default. A good credit rating means a borrower is more reliable and at lower risk of defaulting on a loan.

Credit Risk

The risk that a bond issuer will default on repayment of the bond.

Creditor

A person or company to whom money is owed. See Lender.

Cross Currency Pairs

A currency pair or transaction that does not involve the U.S. dollar.

Crude Oil

An unrefined fossil fuel or petroleum product composed of hydrocarbon deposits and other organic materials.

Cryptocurrency

A digital asset designed to work as a medium of exchange. Cryptography is used to secure transactions using the currency, and to control the creation of additional units of the currency.

Currency

A medium of exchange for goods and services, usually issued by a government. See Money.

Currency Carry

A trading strategy that involves borrowing at a low interest rate and investing in an asset that provides a higher rate of return.

Currency Peg

A central bank monetary policy that keeps its exchange rate fixed to another country's exchange rate. For example, Panama pegs its currency at an exact 1:1 exchange rate with the US dollar.

Currency Tokens

A type of token that can be used as a medium of exchange, just like money (market terms).

Current Ratio

The ratio between a company's assets and liabilities. A measure of a company's solvency.

Custodian

A financial institution or person responsible for safeguarding a firm's or individual's financial assets.

Custody Fees

A fee charged by brokers for looking after, or safekeeping, securities held on behalf of a client.

Cyclical Stocks

Stocks whose prices rise and fall in accordance with the economic cycle or time of year.

Dapps

Decentralized applications that run on a network of computers, rather than on a single computer, like a normal application. This allows for applications to be run using the processing power of many computers across the world that are digitally connected to a network. These applications form the basis for transactions using cryptocurrencies, many of which are run through blockchain systems.

Dark Web

The internet of websites only accessible by the use of decoders. These decoders allow users to anonymously access websites without their internet service provider or the government being able to track their internet history. The dark web is notoriously difficult for the government to regulate, which is made worse due to the profusion of illegal content on the dark web, including gambling, hacking and drugs.

Day Trading

The buying and selling of securities within a single trading day, using high amounts of leverage and short-term trading strategies to exploit small price movements in highly liquid assets.

Dead Cat Bounce

A market pattern in which a share price has a major fall, then moderately recovers, only to then continue falling again.

Dealer

A company or individual investing their own money by selling or buying assets such as stocks, bonds or currencies.

Debt

Debt is money that is borrowed. It can take many forms, but there are two main categories of debt: taking out loans and issuing bonds.

Debt Equity Ratio

This is a liquidity ratio that compares a company's total debt to total equity. The debt to equity ratio shows the percentage of company financing that comes from creditors and investors.

Decentralized Autonomous Organization (DAO)

An investor-directed venture capital fund built on the Ethereum network that was hacked in June 2016. The hack stole about a third of the DAO's funds and led to Ethereum being hard-forked the following month. The DAO is often cited as one of Ethereum's biggest stumbles thus far.

Decentralized Currency

A currency not issued and overseen by a centralized body such as a government or bank. The aim of creating a truly decentralized currency is a major aim of cryptocurrencies.

Default

The failure of a borrower to complete the repayment, including interest, of a loan.

Deflation

A decrease in the general price level of goods and services. Deflation occurs when the inflation rate falls below 0%.

Delegated Proof of Stake (DPoS)

A proof of stake version that runs democratically, allowing users to vote for other users using tokens. The elected users are then responsible for running nodes, mining blocks, and overseeing the blockchain system.

Delisted

The removal of a security from a stock exchange. This can be done to take a business private or to complete a merger or acquisition. A business may also be delisted due to its failure to meet the requirements of an exchange, bankruptcy or because the business is ceasing operations.

Delisting (Delisted)

The removal of a security from a stock exchange. This can be done to take a business private or to complete a merger or acquisition. A business may also be delisted due to its failure to meet the requirements of an exchange, bankruptcy, or because the business is ceasing operations.

Delta

The rate at which the price of a security changes. For investors, this determines the speed at which a trade makes or loses money.

Depreciation

A decrease in the value of an investment, or the fall in the value of a currency due to market forces.

Depression

A severe, sustained economic downturn. Although they are similar, this is not the same as a recession.

Derivatives

A group of financial contracts that derives its value from the performance of underlying assets such as commodities, indexes, or interest rates. Derivatives include forwards, futures, options, and swaps.

Developed Market

A country with a high standard of living, a well-run stock market, and (mostly) free trade, such as Western Europe, Australia, Canada, Hong Kong, Japan, New Zealand, Singapore, and the United States.

Digital Coin

Money in digital form, also known as a crypto asset or cryptocurrency, that can be used as a way to purchase goods or conduct business online.

Digital Currency

A currency that does not consist of physical coins and notes, but rather is based entirely digitally. This allows transactions to be processed instantaneously and free from the control and oversight of governments and foreign borders.

Digital Currency Exchange

Businesses that allow users to trade digital currencies for other assets, such as conventional fiat money or other digital currencies.

Digital Wallet

A digital or physical address in which a cryptocurrency can be stored, and from which a cryptocurrency can be sent or received during a transaction. Wallets are secured by only being accessible by the use of a private key.

Director

A person who is in charge of an activity, department, people, or an organization.

Dirty Price

The price of a bond, which includes all interest accrued since the last coupon payment.

Dispersion

A measure of how variables behave compared with their average. Typical measures of dispersion include range, variance, standard deviation, and absolute deviation.

Distributed Denial of Service (DDoS)

A digital attack that uses large numbers of computers under the attacker's control to overload a network, resulting in the network being overwhelmed and unable to provide its normal service to users.

Distributed Ledger

A record of data that is spread across multiple computers and networks, all of which digitally share the responsibility of sharing and approving data entries. This results in a full record of data being stored across many different computers, each of which has full access to the data and can confirm the data on another computer is correct.

Diversification (Diversified)

A strategy for lowering portfolio risk by spreading investment over several different asset classes, decreasing the potential losses following market downturns for individual asset classes.

Dividend

A portion of a company's net income that is distributed amongst shareholders, rather than being invested back into the company. Some companies pay no dividends at all, and instead re-invest all profits. The portion of a company's net income paid out as dividends reflects its generosity.

Dividend Yield

A measure of the size of a dividend, which is found by expressing the dividend as a percentage of a share's current price. The dividend yield reflects a company's generosity.

Dual Listing (DLC)

A listing of any security on two or more different exchanges. For instance, it is quite common to see a non-US company listed on its own stock exchange and in the US as an ADR.

Duration

The approximate change in a bond's price as interest rates move. This is the bond-specific term for Delta.

Earned Income

Money derived from paid work.

Earnings

After tax net income or a company's profit.

Earnings Beat

The event in which a company's quarterly earnings exceed its earnings estimate, which is the level of earnings analysts expected. A company that beats earnings estimates is considered to be outperforming its peers.

Earnings Estimate

An analyst's estimate for a company's quarterly or annual earnings per share (EPS). Earnings estimates are arguably the most important data points when attempting to value a company, as they are indicators of a company's size, growth, and profitability.

Earnings Per Share (EPS)

An indicator of a company's profitability. It is calculated by dividing a company's net income by its total number of shares.

EBITDA

A company's earnings before interest, taxes, depreciation and amortization are subtracted.

Economic Cycle (Cycles)

The natural fluctuation of the economy between periods of expansion (growth) and contraction (recession). Factors such as gross domestic product (GDP), interest rates, levels of employment, and consumer spending can all help determine the current stage of the economic cycle.

Economic Growth

An increase in the size of the economy as a result of an increase in at least one of three factors: household spending, government spending, or business investment.

Economy

All of the business activity in a given region. The size of the economy is based on the levels of production, the consumption of goods and services, and the supply of money.

Elliot Wave

A technical analysis tool used by analysts and traders to analyze market cycles and trends by identifying extremes in investor psychology, highs and lows in prices, and other factors.

Emerging Market

A country that is progressing toward becoming a developed market, usually by means of rapid growth and industrialization. The countries in the BRIC group are considered the leading emerging markets, and include Brazil, Russia, India, and China. Other major emerging markets include South Korea, Mexico, Indonesia, Turkey, and Saudi Arabia.

Entrepreneur

Someone who starts a new business. Entrepreneurs face a great deal of risk in starting a new business, but this risk can result in massive rewards if the business is successful.

Equity

The stake that shareholders have in a company. Selling equity is one of the main ways for a business to raise money for growth, along with borrowing.

Equity Capital Market

An investment banking division responsible for helping companies raise financing by selling equity in their business to new shareholders. The ECM division structures the issuing and helps set a target price for new shares.

Equity Funding

A way for businesses, especially new businesses, to raise money by issuing equity in their company. Shares of the business are sold to investors in exchange for money, giving the business money to spend on growth, and giving the investors a stake in the company.

Equity Market (Stock Market, Equity Capital Market)

A market in which stocks and shares are issued and traded through exchanges or over-the-counter markets.

Equity Token

A token that grants its holder equity in an organization or business. In this way, equity tokens essentially act as crypto stocks.

Escrow

A transaction method in which a third-party collects the assets being exchanged between the two parties to a transaction. Once both parties agree that the third-party has successfully collected all of the assets to be exchanged, the third-party then distributes the assets that each party expects to receive in the transaction.

Ethereum

An open software platform based on blockchain technology that enables developers to build and deploy decentralized applications. Ether is the cryptocurrency generated by the Ethereum platform.

Ethereum Virtual Machine (EVM)

The platform for Ethereum smart contracts and transactions, which is run by every node in the Ethereum network.

Exchange Traded Fund (ETF)

Unlike mutual funds, which are traded only once a day after the market closes, Exchange Traded Funds or ETFs are a basket of securities that trade on an exchange throughout the day, just like a stock.

Exchange Traded Note (ETN)

Unsecured debt securities that track the performance of a securities index and are traded on exchanges. They are similar to bonds but do not pay out interest. Instead, the prices of ETNs fluctuate like stocks

Executing Broker

A broker that processes a buy or sell order on behalf of a client.

Export

A good or service sold between countries in trade. The country selling the good counts it as an export, which increases their trade balance and grows their economy. This good counts as an import for the other country.

FAANG

Acronym for the biggest and best-known tech stocks: Facebook, Apple, Amazon, Netflix and Google.

Factors

Characteristics, or signals, that can explain why a price goes up or down for a particular instrument. The signals are normally derived from a securities underlying data fundamentals.

Fantasy Finance

An Invstr game where the aim is to maximize the performance of your investment portfolio and win prizes.

Faucet

A site that gives away free coins to its users, usually in exchange for completing simple tasks or clicking on advertisements.

Fear of Missing Out (FOMO)

The overwhelming sensation people get when the price of an asset they don't own starts to skyrocket.

Fear, Uncertainty and Doubt (FUD)

Baseless negativity spread intentionally by someone that wants the price of something to drop.

Federal Deposit Insurance Corporation (FDIC)

An independent federal agency that insures clients' deposits in US banks in the event of bankruptcy.

Federal Funds Rate

The interest rate that US banks charge other banks for lending them money from their reserve balances on an overnight basis.

Federal Open Markets Committee (FOMC)

A committee within the Federal Reserve charged with overseeing open market operations, such as the buying and selling of US Treasury securities. The FOMC regulates the supply of money that is deposited in banks and available to lend to businesses and consumers.

Federal Reserve (The Fed)

The United States' central bank, which is responsible for setting all monetary policy, including money supply and interest rates.

Fiat currency (Fiat)

Any form of physical paper currency that is both regulated and centralized; namely, most national currencies of the world.

Financial Analysis

The evaluation of the financial performance, position, and prospects of a business. Typical financial analysis techniques include risk analysis, cost analysis, and calculating the rate of return and return on investment.

Financial Industry Regulatory Authority (FINRA)

An independent regulator securities firms doing business in the United States.

Financial Institution

An establishment that conducts and oversees financial transactions such as investments, loans, and deposits. These may include commercial banks, central banks, investment banks, and investment funds.

Financial Markets (Markets)

A market in which people trade financial securities and derivatives.

Financial Ratios

The numbers taken from the balance sheet, income statement, and cash flow statement that are used to perform quantitative analysis to assess a company's liquidity, leverage, growth, margins, profitability, rates of return, and valuation.

Financial Regulation

A form of supervision by governments and central banks that ensures that financial institutions adhere to certain requirements, restrictions and guidelines, all of which aim to maintain the integrity and stability of the financial system.

Financial Statements

Documents used by investors to evaluate a company's financial health and earnings potential. The three main financial statements are the balance sheet, the income statement, and the cash flow statement.

Financial Technology (FinTech)

A business sector comprised of companies that aim to provide financial services through the use of software and modern technology.

Fintech Disruptor

A new business in the financial sector that uses cutting-edge internet-based and mobile technology to create new and superior banking products and services that revolutionize the field.

Fiscal Policy

The means by which a government adjusts its spending levels and tax rates to guide and stabilize a country's economy.

Fiscal Year

The period over which companies produce their annual reports. Fiscal years are a year-long, but are not required to line up with a calendar year. Each fiscal year consists of four quarters.

Fixed Income (FI)

A type of security, also known as a bond or money market security, that is a loan made to a government or corporate borrower.

Fixed Peg

A system in which a currency's value is pegged or fixed to a larger currency at a set exchange rate. This rate remains constant over time, and can only be changed by the Central Bank, which will only change the peg in exceptional circumstances. For example, Panama pegs its currency at an exact 1:1 exchange rate with the US dollar.

Floating Rate Note (FRN)

A bond whose coupon rate is variable as it is tied to a benchmark rate, such as LIBOR or the US Treasury Bill rate.

Follow-On Offering

A sale of stock by a company or shareholder that is already publicly held. Also known as a Secondary Offering.

Foreign Exchange Market (FX)

The over-the-counter market in which the foreign currencies of the world are traded. It is considered the largest and most liquid market in the world.

Foreign Exchange Rate (Exchange rate)

The price of a country's currency stated in terms of another country's currency.

Fork, Hard Fork

The permanent divergence of an alternative operating version of the current blockchain. Forks come into existence when a 51% attack occurs, a bug in the program arises, or more commonly, a new set of consensus rules come into existence. These happen when a development team creates and inserts notably substantial changes into the system. The successful fork is decided by the height of their blocks. (You can think of it as a stock split!)

Forward

A non-standard futures derivative contract where the buyer agreeing to buy at a future date takes a long position, and the seller takes a short position.

Forward foreign exchange deal

An agreement to exchange a particular amount of two currencies on a set date at an agreed-upon exchange rate.

Forward Outright

An agreement to exchange a particular amount of two currencies on a set date at an agreed-upon exchange rate.

Forwardation

A situation in which the futures price of a commodity is greater than the expected price on the maturity date of the contract. It's also known as Contango.

Fractional Investing (fractional trading)

A method of investing by which investors can buy fractions of whole shares, meaning they do not need to buy an entire share of a company to invest in it. Through Invstr+, you can begin investing through fractional shares with as little as $1!

Friendly Takeover

A takeover that is agreed upon between two companies prior to the takeover going through.

FTSE

A share index of the 100 companies with the largest market capitalizations listed on the London Stock Exchange. Also referred to as The Financial Times Stock Exchange Index, FTSE 100 Index, FTSE 100, FTSE, or, informally, the 'Footsie'.

FUDster

Someone who is spreading FUD!

Full Node Validation

A program that fully validates transactions and blocks using nodes.

Fund of Funds

A collective investment fund that invests in other funds, rather than investing directly in individual securities.

Fund Manager

An investment professional who oversees the investments within a portfolio.

Funding

Putting money into an account or other such form of deposit.

Fundamentals (market fundamentals)

Financial information that contributes towards the valuation of a company, security, or currency. These can be both quantitative and qualitative, and help investors understand more about its growth and financial wellbeing.

Fungible

An asset that can be directly replaced with other units of the same asset type. For example, gold is a fungible, because an investor can exchange 1 kilogram with another kilogram of gold without changing the value of his overall holdings.

Futures

A financial contract between a buyer and seller that sets a date at which an asset will be exchanged at the market price. Both the buyer and seller are required to honor the contract on the date, even if the market price is unfavorable for both parties.

Gambling

A category of game in which players bet sums of money to win more money. Gambling is often very high risk, with the odds stacked against the players, and is mostly, if not entirely, luck based.

Gas

A measurement of how much processing is required by the network to process a transaction. Simple transactions, like sending ether to another address, typically do not require much gas. More complex transactions, like deploying a smart contract, require more gas.

Gas Price

The amount of ether to be spent for each gas unit on a transaction. The initiator of a transaction chooses and pays the gas price of the transaction. Transactions with higher gas prices are prioritized by the network.

Gearing

The relationship of a company's debt to equity. Measures a company's leverage.

Gilts

UK government bonds, which are considered to be low-risk investments because they are backed by the UK government. They are the UK's equivalent to US Treasuries.

Global Depository Receipts (GDR)

US stocks traded in foreign markets in that country's local currency.

Globalization

The interaction and integration of people, companies, and governments across the globe. It is a process driven by international trade and investment, and greatly sped up by information technology.

Going Long

Buying assets with no immediate intention of selling them, but instead for long-term investment or speculation. Can also mean just buying an asset or security.

Going Short

Selling assets before actually buying them. This happens when an investor believes the price of the item will be lower than its current price. It is the opposite of going long.

Good 'til Cancelled (GTC)

An order given to a broker to buy or sell a security at a fixed price which remains in effect until the investor cancels it or the trade is completed.

Goods & Services

Goods are items that are tangible or physical. Services are activities provided by other people. Together, they are the production, distribution and consumption of goods and services which underpin economies.

Goodwill

The intangible or non-physical assets of a company (such as its brand name, reputation, or popularity) that may add value to a company.

Government

One of the three main players in an economy. Governments decide how much they will spend, as well as the tax rate. In most developed countries, the government is independent from the central bank, which sets interest rates.

Government Spending

Money spent by a government on goods and services such as infrastructure spending and health services, and payment transfers such as state pensions.

Greenback (USD)

A slang term for the US dollar, originating from the American Civil War.

Gross Domestic Product (GDP)

A data point that provides a measure of a country's economic activity. It is the sum of all spending in the country's economy.

Growth (Grow)

Generation of positive cash flows or earnings. A growth company usually has very profitable reinvestment opportunities.

Growth Fund

A diversified portfolio of stocks that has capital appreciation as its primary goal, rather than yield income or dividend payouts.

Growth Stock

A stock for which earnings per share are growing faster than the market average.

Gwei

A denomination of ether. Gas prices are most often measured in Gwei. 1 Ether = 1000000000 Gwei.

Hash

The algorithm that decrypts the data from a block to generate an output, which can then be utilized on the blockchain network. The process of discovering blocks and using this algorithm to solve the blocks is known as mining.

Hash Rate

The rate at which a block's data is decrypted through hashing. Higher hash rates allow for quicker mining.

Hedge

A way of protecting or minimizing risk against financial loss or other adverse circumstances by offsetting a primary investment with an investment in the opposite position.

Hedge Fund

A private investment company that invests its clients' money in a range of strategies to either beat the market or provide a hedge against unforeseen market changes.

Hierarchical Deterministic Wallet (HD wallet)

A type of bitcoin wallet that can generate many different keys from a single parent key. These 'child keys' can be public or private, and allows for the wallet owner to distribute many different keys while keeping the main key private and secure.

High Frequency Trading (HFT, High Frequency Traders)

A trading platform that can process a very large numbers of trades very quickly using powerful computing technology and complex algorithms. It can be used to either find the best price for a single large order, or to find opportunities for profit in the market in real time. HFTs can gain millisecond advantages over rivals and especially retail investors by placing themselves nearby to the exchanges taking orders.

High Net Worth Individual (HNWI)

A wealthy person with investable assets in excess of $1 million.

Holdings

All of the securities possessed within a given portfolio.

Hostile Takeover

A takeover attempt in which the company being acquired did not agree to a takeover, and is resistant to being acquired.

Household

As one of the three main players in an economy, household represents the spending of all individuals in the economy.

Hyperinflation

A term used for excessive, rapidly increasing inflation, which only occurs in extreme cases.

Import

A good or service sold between countries in trade. The country receiving the good counts it as an import, which decreases their trade balance and shrinks their economy. This good counts as an export for the other country.

Income

Money an individual or business receives that they do not need to give back. There are two classes of income: earned income and unearned income.

Income Statement

One of a company's core financial statements, which shows the net income of a company. Also included in the income statement are the company's revenues, costs, profit, and taxes.

Income Stock

A stock that pays out regular and generous dividends to its investors.

Income Tax

The tax imposed on income generated by businesses and individuals.

Indenture

The contract associated with a bond that details the terms and conditions of the bond, including the bond term, interest, and repayment schedule.

Index

A group of securities selected to track a particular investment's rate of return against the market, asset class, sector, industry, or a particular strategy.

Index Constituent

A security that is included in an index, with the aggregate of all the securities making up the index.

Index Fund

A mutual fund or exchange-traded fund that tracks a specified basket of underlying investments such as an index.

Indexing

An investment strategy that seeks to replicate the performance of a certain index by building a portfolio that resembles the set of securities in that index, or by investing in ETFs. Also known as passive investment.

Inflation

An increase in prices and fall in the purchasing value of money.

Initial Coin Offering (ICO)

A way for a new cryptocurrency project to raise money for their project by offering a select amount of coins for sale to the public at a base price. It is the cryptocurrency equivalent of an Initial Public Offering, where stocks are offered for sale in a company about to be listed on a stock exchange.

Initial Public Offering (IPO)

The first public issuance of shares in a company on an exchange. An IPO is often initiated after the company has already raised lots of money through selling shares privately and taking on debt.

Initial Token Sale (ITS)

A way for a new cryptocurrency project to raise money for their project by offering a select amount of coins for sale to the public at a base price. It is the cryptocurrency equivalent of an Initial Public Offering, where stocks are offered for sale in a company about to be listed on a stock exchange.

Insider Dealing (Insider Trading)

A criminal act in which an investor makes profitable trades based on insider knowledge - knowledge that is not public information, and was obtained from an industry 'insider'.

Institutional Investor

A professional investor, usually working on behalf of a financial institution, such as a bank or investment fund.

Instruments (Instrument)

Financial contracts that represent some monetary holdings,

ownership, or promise to exchange, such as equities or debt.

Insurance Company

A business that provides coverage in the form of compensation as a result of loss, damages, injury, treatment, or hardship in exchange for premium payments. An insurance company calculates the risk of occurrence, then determines the cost to pay for the loss to come up with the premium amount.

Intangible Assets

The nonphysical assets of a company, such as its brand name, reputation, or popularity, that may add value to a company.

Interest

The cost of borrowing money. Alternatively, the fee for lending. It is typically expressed as a percentage of the total borrowed or loan amount.

Interest Rate (Rates)

The rate at which a lender charges a borrower interest. Normally expressed as a percentage of the loan amount.

Introducing Broker

A broker that contracts with a clearing firm to handle the execution and settlement of orders that it receives from its clients to buy and sell securities.

Inventory

Backup storages that companies and governments keep to avoid running out of necessary commodities in times of high demand or low supply.

Investing (Invest)

The allocation of funds to a security or providing capital to a business or project with the expectation of generating an income or profit.

Investment

The purchase of assets or securities that will provide income in the future, or will be sold at a profit.

Investment Advisor

A person or organization that receives compensation for providing investment advice, often through managing an investment portfolio on behalf of a client.

Investment Bank

A bank providing financial services to companies, governments, or wealthy individuals. This is in contrast with commercial banks, which provide financial services to the general public.

Investment Company

A corporation or trust that invests the pooled capital of investors in financial securities.

Investment Fund

A pool of capital that a number of individual investors pay into, which is used to collectively invest in stocks

Investment Philosophy

A set of guiding principles that relate to and shape a fund's overall investment strategy.

Investment Strategy

A set of rules to help an investor select an investment portfolio based on certain objectives, risk and skill levels.

Investment Trust

An investment fund which sells its shares on an exchange, allowing investors to invest in the company without having to directly negotiate with the fund to invest their money.

Investor

Anyone who makes an investment!

Invisibles

Assets that are not tangible, but still add financial value to the company. Invisible assets include ideas, intellectual property, and brand recognition.

Invstr Academy

Where learning about investing is fun and easy, and where you can: go at your own pace; test your knowledge with fun quizzes; use the Glossary for easy reference; earn trophies as you complete each module and receive an Invstr Academy certificate when you graduate investa cum laude.

Issue (Issuance, issues, share issuance)

The act of offering securities in order to raise money from investors.

Issue Size

In a bond offering, it is the number of bonds issued multiplied by the face value, or price, of each bond. Also known as the Principal.

Issued Share Capital

The total number of shares in a company currently held by shareholders.

Invstr Unlimited

Subscription offering add-on features including: Full Invstr Academy experience; extra Fantasy Finance trades; XP points; flexible portfolio allocation; technical analysis charts; monthly capital insurance; private trading mode.

Issuer

An entity that issues securities in order to raise money.

John Maynard Keynes

A British economist whose ideas changed the theory and practice of macroeconomics and the economic policies of governments, better known as Keynesian Economics. Considered the most influential economist of the twentieth century, he's most famous for his work on business cycles and the belief that free markets create full employment.

Junk Bond

A high-risk bond that has a high yield, but that comes with a higher risk of default. Junk bonds are often purchased by market speculators and traders who are seeking to make a high return, as opposed to a safer investment.

Keynesian Economics

Macroeconomic theory founded by British economist, John Maynard Keynes, that governments should raise demand to boost growth through spending.

Know Your Customer (KYC)

The process used by businesses to verify the identity of their clients either before or during the time that they start doing business with them.

Lambo

Lamborghini. What we're all going to buy when we're rich!

Legal Tender

Any medium of payment recognized by law.

Lender

A party that provides money to a borrower, which the borrower is expected to repay along with interest.

Lending

The temporary giving of money to someone or a business on condition that it is repaid at some time in the future.

Leverage Buy Out

The acquisition of a company using a significant amount of borrowed money to meet the cost of the acquisition.

Leveraging

A business growth strategy in which money is borrowed to speed up investment. When a company borrows heavily for its investment, it is said to be highly leveraged.

Liabilities (Liability)

What a company owes other parties. Bank debt, mortgage debt, and taxes owed are all examples of liabilities.

Limit Order

An instruction given by an investor to a broker to buy or sell a security at a specific price or better.

Liquidation

The closing down of a company following bankruptcy, in which its assets are sold off to pay off debts to creditors. It can also refer to the forced sale of an investor's brokerage account after a failure to meet a margin call.

Liquidity (Liquid, liquid securities)

The degree to which assets can be sold without substantially affecting that asset's underlying price. Stocks traded on an exchange are typically considered liquid, whereas cryptocurrencies are not.

Liquidity Risk

The risk that a company, bank, or individual may be unable to meet short-term financial demands because of a lack of liquidity in their portfolio. The risk usually arises due to the inability to convert an asset to cash without a loss of money in the process.

List

Where shares in a company can be bought and sold on a particular stock market

Listing

The placement of a company's securities on to an exchange, where it can then be freely traded.

Load

The commission paid on a mutual fund purchase or sale.

Loan

An amount of money that is borrowed, and which the lender expects to be paid back in full along with interest.

Lock limit

A given price at which futures trading is capped, meaning the price of the security cannot rise beyond that limit. Lock limits are put in place to prevent extreme volatility in futures markets.

London Interbank Borrowing Rate (LIBOR)

The short-term rate set by the Bank of England and used worldwide to set the interest rate at which banks lend money to each other. It is gradually being replaced by Sonia (Sterling Overnight Index Average) in the UK and SOFR (Secured Overnight Financing Rate) in the US, following fraud and collusion in the way the rates were set by banks.

Long-Term Interest Rate

An interest rate on an instrument or security with a maturity date longer than one year.

Macroeconomy

The behavior and performance of an economy as a whole. It focuses on the aggregate changes in the economy, such as unemployment, interest rates, GDP, and inflation.

Managed Account

A portfolio of stocks or bonds owned by an individual and managed by a professional investment manager for a fee.

Management Forecasts

An attempt to cope with future uncertainties by analyzing trends from past and present data. Forecasting starts with certain assumptions based on a manager's experience and knowledge.

Mandate (Investment mandate)

An instruction to manage a pool of capital or a fund, using a specific investment strategy.

Margin Call

A demand by a broker that an investor deposit more money or securities into their brokerage account. This occurs when the investor is buying securities using money borrowed from the broker, so the broker makes the investor deposit more money to cover possible losses.

Margin Lending

The borrowing of money to invest, using shares or managed funds as security. It can help an investor increase their returns but conversely magnify their losses, too.

Mark-to-Market (MTM, marking to market)

A realistic appraisal of the value of an investor's portfolio by showing the current market value (usually at the end of day) of the investments. rather than when they were bought. It is also known as a Fair Value.

Market Capitalization (Market Cap)

The value placed by investors on a company. It is calculated by multiplying its share price by the number of shares outstanding. It indicates the size of the company, as well as how much investors believe the company is worth overall.

Market Data

A collective term for the data and information used by the market to analyze trading opportunities and make investments.

Market Drivers

The underlying forces that drive consumers to buy products and pay for services. The most common market drivers are consumer demand and government policy.

Market Economy

A system where the laws of supply and demand (capitalism) direct the production of goods and services. In contrast, socialism and communism apply a command economy to create a central plan that guides economic decisions.

Market Is Always Right

Overall supply and demand controls a market's price movement; an individual cannot influence the market price.

Market Maker

A bank or brokerage firm that provides a firm bid (sell) or ask (buy) price on stocks throughout the entire trading day.

Market Order (Order)

An instruction given by an investor to a broker to immediately buy or sell a security.

Market Price

The price at which an asset or service can be bought or sold.

Markets

A place where two parties or more can exchange goods or conduct other transactions.

Matching Engine

The component of an electronic exchange that matches investors' bids and offers to complete trades.

Maturity

The date by which the issuer of a bond promises to repay the full-face value of a bond, plus interest.

Mean Reversion

The assumption that a stock's price will tend to move to the average price over time. It is a trading method commonly applied by market participants that are big enough to move a market price.

Mergers & Acquisitions (M&A, merger, acquisition)

A term for the group of transactions in which a company joins together with another company (a merger) or is bought by another company (acquisition).

Microeconomy

The study of individuals, households and firms' behavior in decision making and allocation of resources.

Miners

Users or network nodes that carry out tasks in order to be rewarded with cryptocoins. The tasks include validating 1MB worth of transactions and identifying a unique hash or digital hexadecimal number.

Minimum Wage

The minimum amount of remuneration that an employer is required to pay wage earners for the work performed during a given period.

Mining

Discovering and solving blocks along the blockchain. A reward is given for solving the algorithm and lengthening the chain, called a block reward. The block reward for the Bitcoin blockchain is paid in Bitcoin.

Modified Duration

The approximate change in a bond's price as interest rates move. This is the bond-specific term for Delta.

Momentum

A measure of the rate of change of the price of an instrument from one period to the next.

Momentum Stock

Stocks that have had high returns over the last three to twelve months.

Monetary Policy

The macroeconomic policy set by central banks in order to keep the economy strong and stable. The main monetary policy tools of a central bank are changing the base rate and the money supply.

Money (M1, 2, 3)

A medium of exchange that can be exchanged for goods and services on the market.

Money Manager (Professional money manager)

An institutional investor who charges a fee for investing your money. Money managers have regularly been shown to generate lower-than-average returns, which is why we make so much more when we choose to invest ourselves!

Money Market

A market in which short-term debt securities are exchanged. These instruments include money, certificates of deposit, and treasury bills.

Money Supply

The total amount of money circulating in an economy at a given time. The money supply can be increased or decreased by a central bank as part of a change in monetary policy.A market with only one supplier, who can then choose the market price for its goods or services because it has no other suppliers to compete with.

Mooning

A market phenomenon in which the price of a cryptocurrency rapidly increases.

Mortgage

A legal agreement in which a bank lends money to a borrower who is seeking to purchase a property. When the loan is granted, the lender takes the deed to the property as collateral, and then gives the deed back to the owner once the debt is repaid.

Mortgage Backed Security (MBS)

A type of asset-backed security that is secured by a mortgage or collection of mortgages. Typically known as MBS.

Moving Average

A series of price averages over time.

Moving Average Convergence Divergence (MACD)

A technical analysis trend indicator that shows the relationship between two moving averages of prices. Typically known as MACD.

Multi-Channel

A business structure in which the business sells its product through multiple different methods, or 'channels.' For example, Apple is a multi-channel business, because it sells its products both in stores and online. Businesses that sell through only one method are called 'single-channel' businesses.

Multisignature

A verification process requiring more than one signature to approve a transaction. This form of security is beneficial for a company receiving money into their crypto wallet. If a company wants to ensure that one employee doesn't have sole access to a transaction, multisig allows for a transaction to be verified by two separate employees before it's complete.

Municipal Bond (Munis)

A tax-free bond issued by a local government or agency to finance public projects such as roads or schools. It is more commonly known as a Muni Bond.

Mutual Fund

A fund that uses money from investors to invest in stocks, bonds, or other types of securities, and is managed by a fund manager who is paid a fee for deciding what to invest in.

National Association of Security Dealers Automated Quotations (NASDAQ)

The largest electronic securities exchange in the United States, NASDAQ was founded in 1971. It is the home of many of the world's most famous technology companies, including Apple, Google, Microsoft, Oracle, Amazon, and Intel.

National Best Bid and Offer (NBBO)

A Securities Exchange Commission regulation requiring brokers to execute at the best available (lowest) ask price and the best available (highest) bid price when buying and selling securities on behalf of investors.

Net Asset

A company's worth, as calculated by finding a company's total assets and subtracting its total liabilities.

Net Asset Value (NAV)

The value of each share of a mutual fund, which is recalculated each day.

Net Export

The difference between a country's total exports and total imports.

Net Income (NI)

A company's profit after subtracting taxes, interest, and depreciation. Also known as realized profits or the bottom line.

Net Margin

A measure of a company's profitability found by expressing a company's net profit as a percentage of its revenue. Also known as the profit margin, net profit margin, or the net profit ratio.

Net Revenue

The money, income, or sales that a business brings in from selling its goods and services, minus expenses.

Net Sale Price

The price of a service or good after taxes and other costs are deducted.

New York Stock Exchange (NYSE)

The largest equity-based stock exchange in the world, it was founded in 1792. Also known as the Big Board, it is located on Wall Street. It was acquired by the Intercontinental Exchange (ICE) in 2013.

Node

A computer connected to the Bitcoin network. A node supports the network by validating and relaying transactions while receiving a copy of the full blockchain itself.

Nominal Interest Rate

The interest rate of a loan before adjusting for inflation. The interest rate controlled for inflation is known as the real interest rate. These terms are most commonly used when referring to the base rate.

Normal Market Size (NMS)

The minimum number of shares in a company for which a market maker must give a price to buy or sell. For a company with a normal market size of 1,000, a market maker would have to provide a price at which it would be willing to buy or sell at least 1,000 shares.

Notes

An instrument that is a legal document that consists of a promise from a borrower to a lender to repay a debt at a given time. The note details how much the borrower will repay the lender, including the interest that the borrower will add on top of the principal, as well as the date the repayment is due.

Open Market Operation

A central bank system to lower or raise interest rates as part of its monetary policy, by buying or selling securities, typically currencies.

Open Source Software

A type of software that is collaboratively produced, shared freely, published transparently, and developed to be a good for the community, rather than the property of a single company or person.

Operating Profit & Loss-P&L

The profit or loss a company makes from its activity before exceptional items, such as taxes, are factored in. Simply put, it is the company's revenues minus the company's costs.

Options

A derivative instrument that gives the holder the right to buy or sell at a prior stated price within a specified timeframe, after which the contract expires. Call options allow the holder to buy the asset. Put options allow the holder to sell the asset.

Ordinary Shares

A share or stock, sometimes called a Common Stock, entitling its holder to vote in AGMs and receive dividends at the company's discretion.

Organic Growth

The expansion of a business through internal growth. For example, organic growth may be driven by expanding the business's product range, number of business locations, and business output. Growth that is not considered organic includes growth through mergers, acquisitions, and takeovers.

Oscillator

A technical analysis indicator that can be used to analyze a security that does not have a clear price trend, usually because its price has been volatile. The oscillator can then find whether the security is currently being overbought or oversold.

Outright Forward

The simplest type of forward foreign exchange contract. It allows the investor to buy or sell a currency either on a specific date in the future or within a range of dates.

Over the Counter (OTC)

A term to describe trades conducted between two private parties independently, rather than through an exchange.

Par Value

The face value of a bond as opposed to its market value.

Passive Fund

An investment fund that simply follows a market index by buying all of the stocks in that index. The holdings of the fund's portfolio only change when the stocks in the tracked index change. This is the opposite of an actively managed investment fund.

Passive Investment

An investment strategy that seeks to replicate the performance of a certain index by building a portfolio that resembles the set of securities in that index, or by investing in ETFs.

PE Ratio (PER)

The ratio of a company's stock price to its earnings per share. It's used to calculate the current value of a company's shares and reflects the expected growth of a company.

Pension Fund

An investment fund or superannuation into which members pay contributions in order to build up a lump sum income for their retirement. They are normally run by insurance companies and a small section of asset managers. They are by far the biggest investors in listed and private companies.

People

Humans within a group such as a country, community or ethnic group.

Performance

The payoff of an investment over a given time, commonly expressed in terms of the rate of return.

Perpetuals

A bond with no maturity date. Also commonly known as a Perp.

Politician

A person actively involved in the business of government.

Ponzi Scheme

Any investing scam or fraud that promises high returns for little risk to the investor. It is named after Charles Ponzi who gained notoriety for swindling people in 1920's USA.

Portfolio

All of the different investments that someone owns. This can include stocks, real estate, cars, wine, bonds, and more. It can either be managed by you personally or an advisor, but should always be diversified and in line with your investment strategy and risk tolerance.

PoSA (PoSA)

A proof of stake variance where transactions are 'cloaked' by other users who, in turn, receive a reward for helping to anonymize the transaction.

Position

The amount of a particular security held by an investor in their portfolio.

PoST (PoST)

A proof of stake variance where, instead of using the amount of coins to calculate age, the period of time the coins have been held at the specific address is used. This method is implemented to avoid making the rich, richer, which many Proof of Stake methods do.

PoSV (PoSV)

A proof of stake variance that rewards users based on how many coins they have and how actively they use them.

Power & Gas

Gas is extracted from gas deposits around the world, liquefied and shipped or piped to power plants to generate electricity.

Precious Metal

A rare and expensive naturally occurring metal such as gold, silver, platinum, and palladium.

Preferred Stock

A type of stock that gives the holder preference over common stockholders. This means that, if the company is liquidated, the company's assets will first be distributed to preferred stockholders to ensure they are fully paid back before any assets are given to common stockholders.

Price

The amount of money given for the payment of a product or service.

Price Action

The movement of a security's price over time.

Price Ceiling

A situation when the price charged is at equilibrium with the price determined by the market forces of demand and supply.

Price Change

The difference in the trading price of a security from one point in time to another. It can also mean the price difference between the daily open and close.

Price Control

A regulation establishing a maximum price to be charged for specified goods and services, especially during periods of war or inflation.

Primary Market

Where securities are first issued. It's the capital market where businesses sell, or float, new stocks and bonds for the first time.

Primary Sale

Where securities are first issued. It's the capital market where businesses sell, or float, new stocks and bonds for the first time.

Principal

In a bond offering, it is the number of bonds issued multiplied by the face value, or price, of each bond. Also known as the Issue Size.

Private Company

A firm held in private ownership and not publicly listed or traded on an exchange.

Private Equity (PE)

A high risk, high return investment fund holding large stakes in illiquid companies. Private equity funds make money by making companies in their portfolio more profitable, increasing the value of the company's shares.

Private Key

In cryptocurrency, the private key is the secret key that only the holder of a wallet should know, as it can allow access to the funds stored on the wallet.

Privatization

The process of moving assets owned by the government into the private sector, where they are under business ownership and control.

Procyclical

When the actions of a measurable product or service move in tandem with the cyclical condition of the economy.

Product

Goods or a service that is sold to customers or other businesses.

Production Cost

All of the costs a business must pay to produce a product or provide a service. These may include supplies, labor, rents, and more.

Profit

The financial gain of a business, which is equal to revenue minus costs. This is calculated before tax: after subtracting taxes from profit, a company finds its net income, which is also known as realized profit.

Profit Margin

A measure of a company's profitability found by expressing a company's net profit as a percentage of its revenue. Also known as the net margin, net profit margin, or the net profit ratio.

Proof of Activity (PoA)

An alternative to proof of stake that compliments a Proof of Work by randomly selecting a group of users from the network to validate a new block. This process helps prevent 51% Attacks, which occur when a user or group controls 51% or more of a network's mining hash rate.

Proof of Burn (PoB)

A method of proving that a user has burned some of their coins in the process of sending a transaction to an address. This method only works with coins mined from Proof of Work crypto currencies. Users will try to burn the most amount of coins to hopefully "win" a block reward.

Proof of Capacity (PoC)

Proof of Capacity, or Proof of Space, uses hard drive mining to validate new blocks. Proof of work miners burn resources whereas proof of capacity allows miners to use space on their hard drives.

Proof of Importance (PoI)

A proof of stake variance where each account is assigned an importance score that proxies its aggregate importance to the economy. This method helps make sure that all the computers on the network agree with each other and can stop people from spending coins they do not have. Users who are "important" can "harvest" and earn rewards.

Proof of Reserves (PoR)

Proof of Reserves is the process by which the issuer of any asset-backed, decentralized, digital token proves that all tokens that have been issued are fully reserved and backed by the underlying asset

Proof of Stake (PoS)

Proof of stake has been considered the greener alternative to PoW. Where PoW requires the prover to perform a certain amount of computational work, a proof of stake system requires the prover to show ownership of a certain amount of money, or stake.

Proof of Storage

A proof of stake variance where the network uses a 'blocktree.' So instead of seeing every single transaction listed a user only sees transactions relevant to him or her. Each node on the blocktree contains a blockchain. As of right now, there is no known practical publicly verifiable proof of storage.

Proof of Work (PoW)

Proof of work was a concept originally designed to sieve spam emails and prevent DDOS attacks. A proof of work is essentially a datum that is very costly to produce in terms of time and resources, but can be very simply verified by another party. The proof of work for Bitcoin is referred to as a 'nonce,' or number used only once. This has been considered an energy intensive alternative to proof of stake, as the computers unfortunately have to be on and running, which also drives the market towards centralization of hashing power. This is what the blockchain aims to defeat!

Proprietary Trading

An investment strategy where a bank uses its own money for trading and investment, rather than trading on behalf of its clients. It is more commonly known as Prop Trading.

Prospectus

A document issued when a new security is first offered for sale. It provides full disclosure of all legally required information about the security.

Public Key

In cryptography, a public key is a key that can be utilized by any party to encrypt a message. Another party can then receive the message and, using a key that is only known to that individual or group, decode the message.

Pump and Dump

The recurring cycle of an altcoin getting a load of attention, leading to a rapid price increase and then followed by a huge crash

Purchasing Power

The amount of goods or services that a certain amount of money can buy at a given time. The result of a decrease in purchasing power is known as inflation, and an increase in purchasing power is known as deflation. Fiat currencies are traded on FX markets based on their respective purchasing powers at that given time.

Put Option

A financial contract that gives an option seller the right, but not the obligation, to sell a security at a specified price within a specific time period.

QR Code

A two-dimensional bar code that can consist of a geometric code contained in one square, which has smaller squares in the top corners and the bottom left corner. They are a popular way of sending public keys in cryptocurrency.

Qualitative Research

Analysis based on the quality of a company with emphasis on

the company's products, services, management, and competitors in order to find a company's competitive advantages.

Quantitative Research

Analysis based on a company's income statements, balance sheets, and cash flows, and the relationship between price and intrinsic value. Current valuations are compared to historical valuations and other similar companies.

Quantitative Easing

An unconventional form of monetary policy which involves a central bank buying back government bonds in order to inject liquidity, or cash, back into the economy. This way, it hopes to increase the money supply and encourage more lending and investment.

Quarter

A three-month period in a company's financial calendar, when financial reports and dividend payments are released.

Quoted Currency

The second currency displayed in a foreign currency pair. It's also called the counter currency. For example, with USD/CAD, the Canadian dollar is the quoted currency.

Rangebound

Where a security price is stuck in a channel between upper and lower limits.

Rate of Return (RoR)

The profit on an investment, expressed as a percentage term.

Real Estate

Property made up of land and buildings.

Real Rate of Return

The rate of return adjusted for inflation.

Realized Profits

A profit that has been turned into cash, as opposed to just being a profit 'on paper' or a marked-to-market profit.

Rebalancing

A process by which a portfolio's original desired level of asset allocation is realigned through the buying or selling of assets. For example, a common investment ratio is 60% stocks and 40% bonds, so investors will sometimes sell off assets and buy others in order to return to this ratio.

Recession

Two consecutive quarters of negative economic growth.

Refinancing

A process by which a company raises new debt in order to pay off existing debts.

Registrar

A bank or trust company responsible for keeping the register of bond and shareholders after an issuer has publicly offered securities.

Regulation

A form of supervision by governments and central banks that ensures that financial institutions adhere to certain requirements, restrictions and guidelines, all of which aim to maintain the integrity and stability of the financial system.

Regulation T

A set of rules that govern investors' cash accounts and the amount of credit a broker or dealer can extend to them for the purchase of securities.

Regulatory Agency (Regulator)

Organizations responsible for the regulation, supervision and oversight of financial services, including markets and institutions, with the aim of providing financial stability, efficiencies and consumer protection.

Relative Strength Index (RSI)

A momentum indicator that measures the extent of a security's price change to evaluate overbought or oversold conditions.

Repo

A form of short-term borrowing of securities or cash against securities, where a dealer sells a security with an agreement to buy it back in the future at an agreed price. The dealer selling the security is effectively borrowing money against the securities. The counterparty who is buying the securities with an agreement to resell them at a later date is in effect lending money.

Reputational Risk

The potential for negative publicity, public perception, or uncontrollable events to have an adverse impact on a company's reputation, thereby negatively affecting its revenue.

Reserve

Assets, such as cash or stocks, that a company has saved up for use at a later time.

Resistance point

The price level beyond which investors are reluctant to buy the instrument.

Return on Equity (ROE)

A company's net income as a proportion of its total equity. It is a measure of how well a company uses investments to generate earnings growth.

Return on Investment (ROI)

The gain or loss generated by an investment relative to the amount of money invested. For example, if an investment of $100 generated $120, its ROI would be 20%.

Returns-return

The expected net income of an instrument over a given period, expressed as a percentage of the initial price of the instrument.

Revenue

The money, income, or sales that a business brings in from selling its goods and services.

Revenue Growth

The increase or decrease in a company's revenue between two periods.

Reverse Stock Split (Reverse split)

A corporate action whereby a company reduces the number of issued shares by combining multiple shares into one, in order to increase the value of its stocks.

Reverse swap

A swap that restores an earlier investment position. For instance, swapping Dollars for Pounds when it benefits an investor's strategy, then reverse swapping the pounds back to dollars when that becomes advantageous.

Reward value

The total value of a block reward. The reward value of the block is usually dependent on the block height.

Rights Issue

A corporate action whereby a company offers its existing shareholders the chance to buy additional shares at a discount price.

Ring signature

A type of signature that can be performed by anyone who has the right key. A group of users will each have the key to sign with a ring signature, and when a signature is required, any given member of that group can sign. Ring signatures are also anonymous, so it cannot be seen which member of that group gave the signature.

Risk

The possibility that an investment will not perform as expected by an investor, and could potentially result in a loss of money. As such, every investor must determine what level of risk is acceptable, recognizing that the higher the expected return, the greater the risk.

Risk Averse

An investor who opts for lower risk investments.

Risk Management

The practice of identifying potential risks in advance, analyzing them, and taking precautionary steps to reduce or curb the risk.

Risk Rate

The rate of return needed to attract equity or loan capital to an investment project.

Risk Reward Ratio

A process of comparing the potential risks and rewards of a decision to determine whether an action should be taken. All investments and decisions have associated risks, so investors and businesses seek out investments that maximize rewards while minimizing risks.

Risk Tolerance

The degree of risk that an investor is willing to take on in order to gain higher rewards. It is critical that all investors understand the extent to which they are comfortable with taking on risks in exchange for potential rewards, and plan their portfolio accordingly.

Robo Advisor

A platform providing automated algorithm-driven financial planning services with very little human supervision. It offers advice and automatically invests a client's assets using information it gleans from an online survey the client is required to complete.

Rolling settlement

The completion of a trade a number of days after the actual transaction took place, typically the day after, or T+1.

Rule of 72

A simple way of determining what returns are needed to double an investment over a chosen period: dividing 72 by the number of years selected defines what annual percentage return is needed to double your money.

S&P500, Standard & Poor's 500 (SP500)

An American stock market index based on the market capitalizations of 500 large companies listed on the NYSE, NASDAQ, or the CBOE BZX Exchange.

Satoshi Nakamoto

The anonymous identity of the founder - or founders - of Bitcoin. The identity of the true developer(s) remains a mystery, and it is believed that they own one million Bitcoins.

Saving

Money not spent. Saving includes putting money aside in a bank account, a pension plan, or just in a wallet!

Savings Account

A bank account in which the bank pays the account owner interest on money that is deposited into the account.

Secondary Market

Also known as the aftermarket, the market on which securities are traded after the initial issuing of the security. When securities are first issued, they are sold on the primary market.

Secondary Sale

Also known as the aftermarket, the market on which securities are traded after the initial issuing of the security. When securities are first issued, they are sold on the primary market.

Sector

One of the areas whereby the economy of a country is divided.

Securities

A tradable financial instrument with monetary value.

Securities Exchange Commission (SEC)

A US regulatory government agency that oversees securities transactions, activities of financial professionals, and mutual fund trading to prevent fraud and intentional deception.

Securities Investor Protection Corporation (SIPC)

A not-for-profit organization that protects an investor's assets with a broker, in the event of its bankruptcy.

Securitization

The process of turning something into a security. For example, securitization includes the process of combining mortgage debts to create a tradable security.

Segregated Witness (SegWit)

The process by which the block size limit on a blockchain is increased. This is accomplished by removing signature data from past transactions.

Self-Regulated Organization-SRO

An organization formed to regulate certain professions or industries. They are usually non-governmental organizations aimed at setting rules of conduct. The two major American financial SROs are the Securities Exchange Commission (SEC) and the Financial Industry Regulatory Authority (FINRA).

Sell Side

The set of financial institutions that sell investment services and assets. The sell-side includes brokers, dealers, investment banks, and investment research and advisory companies.

Settlement

The completion of a trade. A trade is settled when the deal has been done, cleared, and the exchanged assets have been transferred between the seller and buyer.

SHA 256

A 'secure hash' algorithm designed by the National Security Agency which is used in several different parts of the Bitcoin network. SHA-256 is used both in the hashing process of mining new blocks, as well as for creating public keys for transactions.

Share Capital

The portion of a company's financial capital that was raised by selling shares to investors.

Share Classes

Designations applied to shares that classify them into different types, each with their own class-specific benefits and drawbacks. There are three main share classes: Class A, Class B, and Class C.

Share Option

A contract that gives an investor the right to purchase shares in a company at a certain price on a given date.

Share Premium

Also called capital surplus, appears on a company's balance sheet as the amount the corporation raises on the issue of shares in excess of their nominal value.

Share Price

The price of a single share or stock trading in the market.

Share Purchase Agreement

A legal contract between a buyer and a seller, or purchaser and vendor, in which the seller sells a stated number of shares at a stated price.

Shareholder

An individual or institution that owns one or more share(s) in a company.

Shareholder Equity (SE)

The net value of a company, or the amount of money that would be returned to shareholders if all of the assets were liquidated and all of the company's debt paid off.

Shareholder Register

A list of owners of a company's shares, updated continuously.

Shares

A unit of ownership in a business, representing an entitlement to the profits of that business.

Shares Outstanding (SHOUT)

All shares of a company currently owned by stockholders. However, this does not include shares owned by the company.

Sharpe Ratio

The performance of an instrument adjusted for risk. A high Sharpe Ration would indicate that the return is very high relative to the risk taken.

Short position

Selling assets before actually buying them. This happens when an investor believes the price of the item will be lower than its current price. It is the opposite of a long position.

Signature

The mathematical operation that lets someone prove their sole ownership over their wallet, coin, or data. These are only known to the owner and are basically mathematically impossible to uncover.

Silk Road

A notorious Dark Web marketplace shut down by the FBI in 2013 which allowed users to exchange Bitcoins for items, many of which were illegal.

Simplified Payment Validation (SPV)

A method for verifying if particular transactions are included in a block without downloading the entire block. The method is used by some Bitcoin clients to verify transactions without having to use as much computing power as normal.

Single-Channel

A business that sells its product through only one method, or 'channel.' For example, a local butcher is a single-channel business, because it only sells its products in-store. Businesses that sell through multiple methods are called 'multi-channel' businesses.

Smart Contract

An unalterable agreement stored on the blockchain that is akin to a real-world contract. Once signed, it can never be altered. A smart contract often defines certain computational checkpoints that have to be met in order for money or data to be transacted, and can even be used to verify things such as land rights.

Soft Commodities

Agricultural products that are grown such as coffee, cocoa, sugar, corn, wheat, soybean, fruit, and livestock.

Solvency

A measure of a company's ability to repay the debts it owes, based on how much money it is earning, spending, and saving.

Sovereign Wealth Fund (SWF)

A state-owned investment fund that is typically used to benefit the country's economy, and funded from surplus reserves. Some of the biggest SWF's are from oil-rich countries.

Spark Spread

The difference between the wholesale market price of electricity and its cost of production using natural gas.

Specialization

A process in which a country opts to focus on producing the good(s) it is best at producing, then trading them with other countries for an array of different goods. This maximizes efficiency, and is why trade is beneficial to the global economy.

Speculation

An investment strategy that seeks very high returns from high-risk investments. These investments are subject to brief but large fluctuations in price, meaning the investment will either gain or lose value at a high rate.

Spending

Money that is given away to other individuals or businesses that we do not expect to get back.

Spinoff

A new, independent company that is established from a branch or division of an existing company. This is often accomplished by the parent company selling off its ownership in the spinoff company by selling shares of the spinoff company.

Spot Trade

A trade that is settled immediately as opposed to a point in the future, or Forward.

Spread (Trading spread, bid-offer spread)

The difference between the buy (bid) and sell (ask) prices of a particular asset, or the difference in price between two assets.

Stag

A trader who makes opportunistic, speculative trades to turn quick profits.

Stagflation

A combination of economic stagnation (low growth) and inflation. This combination can be devastating to an economy, and is difficult to escape.

Stealth Address

An address to and from which cryptocurrency funds may be sent, but which makes the identity of the user conducting the transaction anonymous to other users on the network.

Stochastic Oscillator

A momentum indicator that compares the price of a security to the range of its past prices over a certain period of time.

Stock Exchange (Exchange, Stock Market)

A market where securities are bought and sold, such as the New York Stock Exchange.

Stock Split

A corporate action whereby a company issues new shares to its existing shareholders, increasing the total number of shares and decreasing the price of shares on the market while leaving the company's market capitalization the same.

Stock Symbol

The abbreviation for a publicly traded security on an exchange. For example, the ticker symbol for Facebook stock is FB.

Stockholder

An individual or institution that owns one or more share(s) in a company.

Stocks

A unit of ownership in a business, representing an entitlement to the profits of that business.

Stop Loss Order

An instruction given by an investor to a broker to buy or sell a security when it reaches a defined price.

Storage

A digital or physical address, such as a wallet, in which a cryptocurrency can be stored, and from which a cryptocurrency can be sent or received during a transaction.

Stress Test

A test conducted by central banks and financial regulators to determine if banks in the economy are fully prepared for a financial crisis or deep recession.

Strike price

The agreed-upon price in the contract of an option, which is the price at which the asset will be exchanged.

Structured Note

A fixed term debt investment made up of two or more derivatives providing a return to the investor if specific conditions are met.

Sub-prime loans

High-risk loans that are given to borrowers with a poor credit history, meaning they are less likely to pay back their loan and are more likely to default.

Superannuation

Money that people pay while they are working so that they will receive payment when they stop, or retire - in other words, a pension.

Supply & Demand (Supply, demand)

A microeconomy term that explains the interaction between sellers and buyers of goods or services. It is best defined as a product (supply) and the desire for that product (demand), and the effect this has on that product's price. High demand and low supply leads to an increase in price of that good, and vice versa.

Support

A market price at which both buyers and sellers are happy to exchange, resulting in price stability around that point. It is the opposite of Resistance Point.

Support point

A market price at which both buyers and sellers are happy to exchange, resulting in price stability around that point. It is the opposite of Resistance Point.

Swap

A contract in which two parties swap financial assets. They are typically traded over the counter, and are usually used to hedge risk against interest rate or currency fluctuations.

Swap Rates

A fixed rate of interest that one party of a swap pays the other in exchange for the cash flow from a floating (not fixed) interest rate.

Swingline Loans

A type of loan that is taken out by companies that require large amounts of borrowing over a very short span. Swingline loans often charge interest rates that are much higher than normal due to the size of the loan and the short period of time the loan is held for.

T+1

A rolling settlement that is completed 1 business day after the transaction was executed.

Takeover

The acquisition of one company by another company. Takeovers are often strategic moves that the purchasing company expects will increase profits. M&A divisions from investment banks often advise both companies during the takeover process.

Tariff

A tax or duty paid on a particular class of imports or exports.

Tax (Taxation, taxes)

A financial charge made by a government on households and businesses in order to fund public services.

Tax Return

A document filed by a business or household detailing its yearly income, so that the government knows how much to tax them.

Tax Revenues

The total income that governments receive from taxation.

Technical Analysis (TA)

The process of analyzing historical graphs and data in order to help make future price predictions about potential investments.

Tenbagger

An investment that increases in value by tenfold (1000%).

Term

The length of time between the issuing of a bond and its maturity date. A bond must be fully payed back, including interest, over the course of its term.

The Flippening

A potential future event when the market capitalization of Ethereum or another altcoin surpasses Bitcoin's market cap, making it the most 'valuable' cryptocurrency.

This Gentleman

"This is it, gentlemen" is a meme used to point out positive things that are currently happening.

Tick

A unit of measure which is the minimum price change of a security. This means that the price of a security cannot change in increments smaller than a tick.

Ticker Symbol

The abbreviation for a publicly traded security on an exchange. For example, the ticker symbol for Facebook stock is FB.

Time Value of Money (TVM)

The greater benefit of receiving money now rather than an identical sum later, due its potential to earn more through interest or investing.

Tokens

A unit of cryptocurrency that serves as a digital representation of an asset, meaning the token could, in theory, be redeemed for gold, or oil, or a new car!

Top Down

An investment strategy based on broad knowledge about the general economic landscape.

Total Return

A measure of an investment's performance that takes into account both the income generated by the investment, as well as the rise or fall in the investment's value. It is expressed as a percentage of the initial investment value.

Toxic Asset (Toxic Debt)

An asset that has fallen in value to such a degree that the market for selling that asset has collapsed.

Trade

An exchange of goods between two parties - normally, in the global economy, this occurs between two countries. Trade is most beneficial when each country specializes in the good it is best at making, as this maximizes efficiency, resulting in goods that are both cheaper and better quality.

Trade Balance

The difference between a country's exports and imports. If a country exports more than it imports, it has a *positive* trade balance; if a country imports more than it exports, it has a *negative* trade balance.

Trade Policy

Sets of laws and policies that seek to change a country's international trade levels or trade balance. Trade policy strategies include tariffs, quotas, taxes, subsidies, and other tools.

Trader

A person who buys and sells securities either for himself or on behalf of another person or institution. Traders differ from investors by holding assets for a shorter period of time to take advantage of short-term trends or patterns. Investors, on the other hand, have a longer-term view.

Trading

An opportunistic way to make a profit by identifying instruments and assets that can be bought and then quickly sold again at a higher price. Although trading is profitable, it is not the same thing as investing, which focuses on growing personal wealth in the long term.

Trading Session (Trading Hour)

The normal trading time in a day excluding any trading that

takes place before the market opening and after the market closes.

Treasuries

Securities issued by the US government that represent debt obligations. Treasury bills, bonds, and notes are all different forms of government-issued security, but each represents an obligation of the U.S. government to repay debt at a certain time.

Trend Analysis (Trends, Trending)

Techniques used to predict the movement of security prices based on historic market data.

Triple Witching

A market event in which three different types of security (stock options, stock index options, and stock index futures) all expire on the same day. Triple witching occurs once per quarter, and creates market volatility due to many traders opening new positions and closing old positions.

Trust

A relationship whereby a trustor gives the trustee the right to hold his property or assets for the benefit of someone else - the beneficiary. It provides legal protection for the trustor's assets, and makes sure those assets are distributed according to the wishes of the trustor.

Ultimate Oscillator

An oscillator (market terms) that uses data from three different time periods to reduce the volatility of the chart. This is especially useful for volatile cryptocurrencies, as it reduces the number of points at which it recommends a trader buy or sell the cryptocurrency, only signaling to buy or sell at the most important points.

Ultra-High Net Worth Individual-UHNWI

A very wealthy person with investable assets in excess of $30 million.

Unearned Income

Income received without working, which may include income from interest, gifts, and prizes.

Unit Investment Trust (UIT)

A type of investment company that has a fixed, unchanging portfolio, which investors can buy shares in. Investors can then redeem these shares for their net asset value at a later date. A UIT has a fixed lifespan, meaning it dissolves on a set date, which is decided upon when the UIT is first established.

Universal bank

A bank offering investment and commercial services to the general public and businesses.

Utility token

A token, often offered by the developers of a cryptocurrency to raise funds, that grants certain privileges to its holder, and allows the holder to perform actions or access resources that are not available without that token.

Valuation

The existing or projected worth of a business or asset.

Value Stock

A stock that trades at a lower price relative to its fundamentals; such as dividend payout, earnings and revenues, thus seemingly looking cheap.

Venture Capital

Financing that investors provide to start-up companies and small businesses that are believed to have long-term growth but, because of their infancy, carry a substantial level of risk.

Volatility (Volatile)

The fluctuation in the price of an instrument over time. If an instrument's price often changes in a rapid and unpredictable manner, it is considered volatile. Volatile instruments can make traders large returns very quickly, but are also extremely risky, as prices can drop suddenly and unexpectedly, leading to large losses.

Trading Volume (VOL)

An indication of how much an instrument is bought and sold over a given time period. Volume reflects the popularity of an instrument.

Volume Weighted Average Price (VWAP)

A price benchmark used by traders and investors to give the average price at which a security has traded throughout the day, based on both volume and price.

Wall Street

The home of the New York Stock Exchange, located in Manhattan in New York City. Also used to refer to the American financial sector as a whole.

Wall Street Crash (Great Depression)

A time in October 1929 when 16 million shares were traded on the New York Stock Exchange in a single day. Billions of dollars were lost, wiping out thousands of investors wealth. Its aftermath led to the Great Depression.

Wallet

A digital or physical address in which a cryptocurrency can be stored, and from which a cryptocurrency can be sent or received during a transaction. Wallets are secured by only being accessible by the use of a private key.

Warrant

A security that guarantees the holder the right to purchase a certain bond or stock at a fixed price in the future.

Watchlist

A list of potential investments an investor wants to watch in order to become more informed about them. The prospective investor will typically watch for the price and volatility of instruments on the watchlist to see if it would be a good investment, as well as the best time to invest in that asset.

Wealth of Nations

The economists bible, written by the father of modern capitalism, Adam Smith. Its radical insight was that a nation's wealth is really the stream of goods and services that it creates.

Wei

The smallest denomination of ether. 1 Ether = 1000000000000000000 Wei (10 to the power of 18)

Whale

Someone who holds a vast amount of a single cryptocurrency.

White Knight

An individual or company who acquires a company by a friendly takeover just prior to the company being acquired in a hostile takeover.

Whitepaper

A document describing the protocol and workings of a cryptocurrency in deep technical detail. It is issued just before the ICO, and includes details about how funds raised in the ICO will be used in the future. Similar to a prospectus (market terms).

Wire Transfer

A method of electronically transferring funds into an account. Also typically called bank transfer or credit transfer.

World Trade Organization (WTO)

The only global international organization dealing with the rules of trade between nations. It superseded the General Agreement on Tariffs and Trade (GATT).

Writer

The party who issues an option and guarantees the terms of the contract.

Yield

The amount earned on a security over a particular period of time.

Yield Curve

A line chart showing the yields of bonds of different maturities with the yield level on the y axis and the maturity of the bonds shown on the x axis. Yield curves can take three shapes: flat, normal, and inverted. A normal yield curve in which the line chart slopes up from left to right shows that bonds with longer maturities have higher yields than bonds with shorter maturities. This is taken as a sign of optimism in the economy. An inverted yield curve in which longer dated bonds have lower yields than shorter dated bonds is taken as a sign of pessimism in the economy or that there might be a recession ahead. A flat yield curve is in between the normal and inverted, and shows that the economy is a transition into either good times or bad times.

Zombie

A company that is unable to stand on its own two feet. In

other words, through a series of bailouts or generous creditors, it earns just enough money to continue operating and service debt, but is unable to pay off its debt.

ABOUT THE AUTHOR

Kerim Derhalli

Kerim Derhalli is the Founder & CEO of Invstr, an award-winning financial education and investment app. Kerim has a thirty-year track record of building, growing and managing multi-billion dollar businesses at leading financial institutions all around the world. His management roles have included Global Head of Equity Trading, Global Head of Index Arbitrage and Proprietary Trading, Global Head of Emerging Markets, Global Head of Commodities and Global Head of eCommerce.

Kerim was awarded 2019 Tech Entrepreneur of the Year - Go: Tech Business Awards, Fintech Innovator of the Year - UK Business Technology Awards, 2018 Fintech Founder of the Year - BMWi Tech Awards, and a 2020 Top 32 Fintech Leader by Business Leader.